January 12, 2002
To a New year
Helen Lewison

Seduction of Silence

Journal of a Reluctant Widow

by

Helen Lewison

Robert D. Reed Publishers
San Francisco

ISBN 1-885003-26-9

Library of Congress Catalog Card Number: 99-066899

Robert D. Reed Publishers
San Francisco

IN MEMORY
OF MY HUSBAND, MEL

"The pipes, the pipes; they are a'calling,
from glen to glen and down the mountain side.
The summer's gold and all the roses dying.
'Tis you, 'tis you must go and I must cry."

From the song: "Danny Boy"

Prologue 1

Finian's Rainbow Revisited

My name is Finian. I want to tell my story. I have resided with two people all of my life, at least all the life I remember. They had been coming to the SPCA looking for someone special. When my master saw me, he hurriedly called my mistress over. She exclaimed, "He is a picture cat, he looks like a picture cat!" They adopted me and took me home.

As a kitten, I would wander back and forth across the couch, first visiting with one of them, then the other. My mistress said I reminded her of a song from Finian's Rainbow:

"When I'm not near the one I love, I love the one I'm near."

Thusly they named me Finian.

My master got sick and went to the hospital. I was very worried. I would go downstairs and look out the window to wait for him to come home. He never did.

My mistress began writing and writing, literally a cloudburst of words! Sheets of paper were flooded with ink marks.

I moved silently about, trying to be loving in my own cat way, hoping that my presence would console her. My master, her mate, died October 16, 1992, and neither of us would ever be the same.

—Finian

Beloved Finian
7-1-81 To 12-31-99

Prologue 2

I write because my father wrote. In the beginning I wrote poetry to please him and he wrote back to please me. As I got older I wrote because circumstances were totally outrageous to the fragile youth I perceived myself to be. And then time passed and strange winds and sounds enabled me to put on paper words, emotions and tears which were never shared.

The continuation of thoughts deep in the night stirred up nightmares; dreams and sound found their way to paper. On and on, life changed, person changed, different cities, different rooms, and they all came together to be assessed and put in their place.

Later rather than sooner, the words began pouring out. Tragedy had set the stage for hundreds of pages of discovery, introspection, speculation, and when the silence around me became seductive, the words began hurtling out of my pen, falling on the floor and were so abundant, I left them there.

Slowly, the rushing subsided and I was safely for the most part in control of the words which had enveloped me; at times to the point of smothering. Now I can write sometimes calmly, sometimes frantically, but I still write. I am grateful; my soul is at rest at least for the time being.

—Helen Lewison

Contents

I SEE RED

November 17, 1992

My husband was in the hospital. He had been there for a long time. He went for a routine operation. The operation went well but he began deteriorating. He was moved to CCU and then to ICU. So many doctors, so many procedures, so many nurses—so many demeaning, insulting tubes. This brave and gallant man was dying and the humiliation of his being reduced to a helpless entity took its toll on me and of course, did ten-fold damage to his dignity. The abuse of dying. I know all the clichés "we all die someday"; "it was his time to go"; the clichés regarding dying are endless. I suppose we have to even out all the clichés of living, i.e., "Do the best you can"; "It all works out in the end."

Let me tell you that dying is not a "cliché." It is real, the most real experience you will ever have—if you are the victim of death or the bedside spouse, child, mother, father, sister or brother of the one who is leaving you forever.

He knew he was dying the last few days of his ordeal and he told me so. His last day, I wore a red blouse—I wanted him to see color. I asked him if he knew what color I was wearing and he nodded "Yes. Red." I held on, I held his hand. I smoothed his brow. I talked about how we would always be together, if not tomorrow it would be soon, and we would spend the rest of eternity with each other. I made plans to be buried with him when my time comes.

"He died," the nurse said peacefully.

When I left him he was asleep with the help of morphine and maybe the touch of my hand on his. I hope he went quietly.

It has been a month since he died. I arranged the funeral at a National Cemetery near my home. A religious service was held in the chapel on the grounds. An Honor Guard of eight young soldiers in full uniform fired their guns. A bugler blew taps and I was handed the American flag. He was my hero. He fought the good fight overseas and was there when World War II ended in northern Germany. He saw

General Montgomery cross the Elbe River to meet the Russian General. The men who served with him so long ago have gone their own way but he talked of them often. They were his family; I think the closest family of his life. They laughed and lived together. They were all young and vital and felt they were doing something absolutely essential in the interest of their country. It all comes down to another cliché "Life is short." I say it is never long enough. I suppose I am still in "shock," but whatever it is, whenever I close my eyes, I see the color red. That was the last color my husband saw and now the color red seems to have become a part of my life. At first, I didn't make the association of why I am seeing red. I am not angry or maybe I am. It is only when my eyes are closed. Is it a dream world where we both see each other through this red haze?

Will it pass? Probably. I had to write about this because it seemed significant. Maybe when I reread this someday, I will come to terms with his death. I hope so.

TOUR OF DUTY

November 20, 1992

I am sixty-eight years. I have served forty-three years on duty. I wonder if anyone has thought of marriage in these terms. I know I didn't.

When you re-enter the world on your own, no more requests, no more admonishments, no more pats on the back, no more compliments—it does seem that you have occupied a strange land all of your life. You cannot focus; it is like walking around without your glasses (I am myopic). Everything is the same but everything is different. The world is blurred and out of sync.

I can do anything at any time I want to do, but what do I want to do? I can go anywhere I want to go, but where do I want to go? I can eat anything at anytime and go to sleep whenever sleep becomes my ally. What and where is the answer?

Marriage is a tour of duty. My life had meaning. There was someone else involved. Without someone to do for and not answer to, how do you start over? Where do you begin? Not really from scratch—I am long past scratch. Do you do as I've been doing? Let the day be, which to me means waking up, having breakfast, feeding my cat and moving in whatever direction necessity aims me or someone calls and I follow the voice. I am not trying too hard to change my days, I wish I didn't feel the sadness, the loneliness that wanders in and out of my days but I accept them as well as the rest of whatever happens in the hours ahead.

I have not made peace with the past and maybe I never will, but as it moves further and further, perhaps I can make some kind of adjustment to it. There will have to be an amicable peace treaty with the past, or the wars within will never be resolved. And I hate war, any war, so maybe I am starting out with one positive aspect. The rest will come, I hope.

The death of one's spouse is so unbelievable. It is not only the shock, the trauma, the sadness, the loss. It is like some part of you has been surgically removed and it's both physical and emotional.

To have lived fully, one has to serve a tour of duty. No matter what problems arose and what joys you experienced, you had this other self. You always knew who you were. You had a mirror to look into and see who you were that day, that moment, or even that year. Now no more mirror and no more "you." It is now time to become your own "you." I am not looking forward to it but I'm not hiding either.

The following from an old nursery rhyme, I just remembered:

"I'm hiding, I'm hiding."
And no one knows where.
For all you can see
Are my toes and my hair.
I just heard my father say to my mother,
"But darling, she must be somewhere or the other."
"Have you looked in the cupboard?"
And mother said "Where?"
"In the cupboard." said father.
But I wasn't there.
"Have you looked in the mirror, that's a pretty good place,"
said mother and looked and saw only her face.
"I'm hiding, I'm hiding."
And no one knows where.
For all you can see
Are my toes and my hair.

WHEN YOU AND I WERE YOUNG, MAGGIE

November 24, 1992

He sits watching TV. He watches for hours—reruns of shows from twenty years ago or maybe a little longer.

He calls to me, "Come look at this actor—how handsome he was and then come look at this actress, she must have been very young, maybe twenty. Wasn't she beautiful."

I know he is not well and can't go out into the world as much as he used to and maybe would still like to, but I am not sure. He is walking backwards in his mind and seeing the past (his own youth, of course, is woven into the fabric of youth and beauty he sees on the screen).

I feel very uncomfortable looking back at these young, beautiful people, who, by now, are either dead or quite old. I am angry, though. I don't voice it often about his preoccupation with these distant figures that are playing out fictitious lives in an imaginary world.

I realize one reason I am disturbed; twenty years ago I was younger, and maybe jealous of youth, not the young of today, but the ones of yesterday.

I want desperately to move forward and enjoy the present and whatever future I have; the past is past; sure I look back and talk about it, but it doesn't envelop me.

I guess he sees no future and the past is his present. I don't want to admit that we will all die someday. I push death away from my thinking. I know it is there waiting for all of us. I feel frozen in time if I can't look forward. He must have sensed his imminent death and wanted to feel even if vicariously, the beauty and warmth of youth. His youth was long ago, and he seemed to mostly remember his dog, Rex. From age thirteen to twenty-three, he and Rex were great friends. They ran around the lake together. They shared so many happy times together. Then boyhood friends, who are long gone, and World War II. He was lucky enough to be witness to the end of the war in Northern Germany when General Montgomery crossed the Elbe River and met the Russian general and closed the gap between the East and the West.

The rest of his life was a pursuit of surviving, working, and he felt he had achieved very little. Not every man sorrows for a lost dream of being "someone of importance," but many do.

I know he was the brightest and most accomplished man I've ever known. He had a great heart which was filled with sadness, and great mind that was filled with anger. The condition of all humanity saddened him and its destiny, including his own, angered him.

I tried to make him laugh and when he did laugh he could fill anyone's heart with joy. Over the years, what little laughter I could evoke from him, became, at best, small smiles.

He's gone now and I miss him, but he's with me in every room in our home. I know how he felt about every picture on the wall and the rugs he walked on and the bed he slept on. This goes on eternally and I know that we are alive as long as someone remembers us, so he will live forever, certainly as long as I live.

He died October 16, 1992.

DREAMTIDE

November 29, 1992

I find myself walking through the halls of a hospital. I go in and out of the rooms. I am looking for my husband. I can't find him.

I take the elevator to another floor and begin my search again. I am in the middle of a dream. My husband died last month. I finally think I see him in a large room. He sees me and comes over. He looks so handsome, healthy and calm.

He says, "It's okay. Death is not so bad, really it's all right."

We walk the halls and talk. He's gentle and soft-spoken.

"Please don't be upset, it's all right; being dead is not what I thought, but I must go now."

I tell him I miss him and he misses me too. He says to take care of myself, but he must go. He walks toward a wall (like we've seen in the movies) and bumps his head.

"I just haven't gotten the hang of it yet!" he says laughing. Then he walks toward the wall again and this time looks back at me smiling and goes through.

I just haven't gotten the hang of it myself. How do I spend the rest of my life without him?

I miss him terribly.

ALL THE KING'S HORSES

5:51 A.M., Saturday, December 26, 1992

"Humpty Dumpty sat on a wall.
Humpty Dumpty had a great fall.
All the king's horses and all the king's men
Couldn't put Humpty Dumpty together again."

You asked me, "Am I going to make it?"

I said, "The doctors say there is no reason you can't."

The doctors were wrong and I was wrong and you were right. You weren't going to make it. I never acknowledged our collective fears which we both hid from each other. You had to make it; I could not even begin to think any other way. I think you were more realistic and just wanted to hear my reassuring words.

From the end of your life to the beginning of the end of my life, I have tried to visualize what that life will be. I know that firstly, love is the top priority. I loved you and always will, but I must go on loving. I cared for you and I must go on caring. I did for you and I must keep on doing. I don't know what form loving, caring and doing will take—it doesn't matter as long as I can accomplish these three things during the rest of my life.

I try to remember books I've read and people I've known. I try to remember places I've been and things I've done. My memories are like dried leaves being swept back and forth with the wind. Fragments of a title, fragments of someone in the past and so it goes. I'll collect the dry leaves as they pass my mind. They give me comfort and awareness as to the next decisions I must make. I'm now walking in an emotional fog and I am fearful— I do not know what I fear, perhaps death or perhaps life.

Now I lay me down to sleep
I pray the Lord, my soul to keep
If I should die, before I wake
I pray the Lord, my soul to take.

RAINDROPS KEEP FALLING

January 7, 1993

I go through all the motions, planning a trip. You died and I'm supposed to go on living. Busy, busy—cruises are easy; there are always lots of people and you don't have to think beyond the next meal, which is prepared for you. You don't have to decide what to do, you have a menu of activities which you can partake of or not. Life is a bowl of cherries aboard a cruise ship. It is elegant, luxurious and you don't even have to get up in the morning if you don't want to.

It was fun planning—which stateroom, which plane flight, buying clothes and then the fun stopped. I will be alone. For the first time in my life, I will be going on a trip alone.

I don't want to go. What is my option? Stay home and wait for your return. You are gone forever, I know that. Wait six months and then make plans.

"You can't make decisions," you said. You're right. Okay, I'm going to prove you wrong.

I am going! Maybe it will be good enough or maybe it will be better than that. You would be proud that I make a decision. I will miss you horribly—I always will, but if it had been the other way around, you would be stuck with the same decision. Do I go on or do I stay walking in place? I hope not. We sleep in the deep forever so I'll just let the raindrops keep falling on my head to make me aware I'm still alive.

REMEMBER WELL

January 10, 1993

"Remember well and bear in mind,
A jaybird's tail sticks out behind."
—Felix

I remember these lines written in a school book printed about the year 1880. Felix was obviously a very brave and courageous boy to write this and sign his name. I wonder what happened to Felix. Did he grow up and go overseas during World War I? Did he marry? Did he have children? I have no idea why this came to mind. I loved to read as a child and how I came to own this book is beyond my memory.

Why Felix, who became so real to me so many years ago, has returned, I have no idea. Maybe it's because I was a "Felix" in my time. The child who did well in school, but could never conform to the status quo. I remember when I was eleven in the sixth grade in grammar school. My teacher was constantly reprimanding me for talking in class. The class was divided into boys on one side and girls on the other. Since I apparently could not contain my verbal skills, she moved me to the boy's side. This did absolutely no good at all.

In a dramatic move, she placed me in the center of the room totally isolated from the girls and from the boys. Even this did not deter me. I just passed notes, to the right and to the left. I have no idea why I needed to reach out and become I am sure to my teacher's dismay—a complete nuisance.

When the year ended, Miss Scruggs (Willie Mae) took me aside and said, "You are a very good student and I hope you will come back some day and tell me what you have done; I really want to know."

I never went back and I really haven't done much except live life the best way I know how; actually I didn't even do that. I sort of let life take me by the hand and followed it through the years.

Yes, Felix, there was this little girl who read your poem and remembers the jaybird.

BY THEIR DEEDS, YOU SHALL KNOW THEM

Wednesday, January 13, 1993

Every book, person or whatever, that tries to console a newly widowed spouse talks about having been half of a couple and the difficult transition to living alone.

I have a different type of transition which might be unique (but probably not). Yes, I was half of a couple , but I was also the whole of the half. It is very hard to define what this means and I will start by saying "I was always me." Yes, we were a couple and we shared many, many things, but I was always me. I was not a half of me. I could take control, I could make decisions (much better when you have the other half to help achieve a more positive solution).

When my husband died, I was left with the reins in my hand. I had to decide where to bury him, what type of funeral, lots of paper work and what to do a few months down the line in order to let the "whole" me continue. It all went so smoothly—to this day almost three months since his death, I find myself wondering how I have accomplished all of this and almost totally alone. The funeral from start to finish, I did alone. Family members attended the funeral and furnished food and there were phone calls of condolences. Then I was alone again.

It's okay. I was always alone, not in the "I'm sorry for myself alone." I contacted insurance companies, social security, filled out forms, made phone calls, all related to my new widowhood; I did it "alone." How could I have been so strong, so capable, so in charge? I have never thought of myself in those terms.

I guess that is part of what I mean when I said I was a whole of a half. I loved being a half of a couple. It was wonderful knowing there was someone always waiting for you and always caring for you unconditionally.

I made plans early on to take my "whole" and start it on its path to the future. I made reservations for a trip to let me "alone" begin my journey into my new life on earth. Of course, I had qualms and misgivings. Yes, there were times I wanted to cancel the trip and not have to face whatever it is that is coming, but the whole me seems to be taking over more and more and I am relying less and less on the half of the whole I was.

I need people, I need friends, I need laughter and I don't kid myself that I am all that self sufficient. I can allow myself to ask for advice, I can allow myself to make mistakes. It is okay. But, you see, I always could. It's just that now that the half is missing I have become aware of the whole I am, and probably have been all my life.

It seems funny to be sitting here patting myself on the back, so to speak. It really isn't that. It is the realization that I've done the best I can in this life and I've made hard decisions. Decisions I'm proud of and that may be I am very lucky that in having been born a whole, I have never lost that identity. I don't really know who I am and probably never will. It really doesn't matter.

Self scrutiny is time consuming and non-productive. The important thing at this time is to keep moving ahead without any specific guidelines—just keep my options open: accept whatever happens, appreciate the warmth of friendship, share the laughter, and only look back to remember. Not sadness, but memories. We all need our memories.

I did it, I did—by my deeds I did!

THE RECOVERY ROOM

January 14, 1993

I've just been through the most devastating operation of my life. The hospital stay was lengthy; three long and arduous weeks. My husband was there commuting between living and dying. I was there. Day after day, totally helpless. Sitting and standing in his room, leaning over his bed, trying to reach him. I took a radio so he could hear music, perhaps to soothe him or comfort him. He took little comfort in these efforts. He wanted me with him but external pleasures were already beyond him. I talked and then it was silent. I talked to nurses, to residents, to volunteer workers, I just talked. Maybe my voice would quell the gnawing fear that the doctors had given up and I was losing him. I never gave up until the doctors gave up, and even then I spent the last day with him.

He kept saying, "Stay, stay..." I watched him leave me, so quietly and gently did he go.

He was a gentle man and as the end came, he left in the quiet with no complaining and the silence was so deafening.

I am slowly beginning to hear again. The sounds around me are slowly taking form. I heard the rain last night, the sun is shining this morning and I am moving among the people of the earth.

I have been in hospitals for surgery myself and when you awaken from the deep sleep of anesthetics, you will find yourself in the Recovery Room. There is always a voice calling your name.

"Helen, Helen... it's over, everything is fine." "Wake up, wake up, it's over... it's over, Helen."

AIR POCKETS

January 16, 1993

I keep hitting air pockets.

The seat belt signs are turned on and a voice over the loud speaker says, "We are experiencing some turbulence. Please keep your seat belts on until further notice."

I've heard this turbulence is also called air pockets. It seems appropriate since you are enclosed in an airplane which seems trapped in a black hole of bumps and thumps.

My life is trapped in an air pocket. My husband died three months ago. I've seemingly moved through time and space fairly smoothly. There have been times of turbulence but they were short lived. Now the turbulence has increased, accelerating at times. I can hear it in my voice when I talk to people; I seem to sound almost hysterical. I guess I'll just have to ride it out and remember that most planes land safely. I just wish it would stop. I hate myself for being afraid. I can cope, I can handle it. I have in the past, of course, I had someone to share my fears with, someone to hold my hand when the plane took off and the plane landed.

I hold hands with strangers now.

DREAMTIME

January 29, 1993

I just woke up. It's very early. I seem to be awakening while it's still dark. Something is very different. As far back as I can remember, I have had nightmares every night. Mostly, I could not remember details but every now and then the dreams that were the most disturbing I would tell my husband and rid myself by sharing.

I don't have nightmares since he died. I still dream and some of them are strange and weird but not a nightmare.

I wonder why my nightmares have, after all these years, so dramatically disappeared. I see my husband lying in the hospital bed during the last week of his life. He looks up at me and says, "I'm dying, I'm dying."

Tears stream down my face. I say, "I don't know where you are going but I promise you that we will always be together, we will always be together." I hold his hand, I touch him—he is so warm and still alive. Now I know where my nightmares went. They followed me into the daylight. They are with me all day, creeping in and out of my consciousness.

My sleep, though brief at night, is relatively peaceful. My days are full of dreams, especially the terrible reality of his death. I spent his last day holding his hand, while he kept saying, "Stay, stay."

He asked if I had eaten. I said, "Yes."

He was still the caring man I had married. I stayed; I stayed but he left me and now I'm living my nightmares. The last thing he said to me was, "Come to bed." I said the bed is too small for both of us.

"I'll come to bed soon," I said.

I had wondered these last few months where my nightmare had gone and now I know. I am living in the *Dreamtime.* Please let the nightmares go back to sleep.

DEATH, THE GREAT LIBERATOR

January 29, 1993

I was gazing out the window. It's a beautiful cool morning with streaking bands of clouds as the sun rises. I feel free, I feel liberated. How ironic, that it takes a death to feel free. Not good, not happy, just free!

I did not realize during all the years of illness, pain, doctor visits and more pain that I would eventually move into the free-zone. Our calendar is filled with dates; dates with doctors, labs, dentists, hospitals and on it goes. Pharmacies, back and forth, medicines, more pills for pain, the back and forth of illness.

Now death has liberated me. My husband is liberated, too. Death took away his pain. Death took away the endless days of worry and anxiety he endured. The days of continual suffering ; he didn't complain, but just said, "I hope you never have to live this way, it would be better to be dead."

At which I would get angry and say, "Okay, if that's what you want."

He said, "Of course, that's not what I want. I want to be with you but not this way."

He got his wish, but I didn't get mine. I would want him here with me forever.

But I'm free. To go to sleep when I'm sleepy, to eat when I'm hungry at any time. No schedules, no guidelines. I'm a little drunk on this freedom, like a prisoner-of-war released after years of imprisonment. I'm giddy on this freedom. I don't really know how to deal with it. I can come and go freely. No one needs me, no one.

At times, I'm breathless, too much fresh air after being interned. Did I feel like I was imprisoned? No, never—when you are with the one you love, there is no confinement, only companionship. How do you deal with this new-found freedom? Slowly, I'm doing whatever I want to do whenever I want to do it. I buy whatever I want to buy, I go wherever I want to go.

If only my heart would quit aching, if only I could feel as joyful as I'm acting. I'm laughing and joining the human race. I'm not really part of the scene but at times, I seem to melt into the big picture. I am alive and I'm free and I'm liberated. I guess that's the sum of it. One way or the other, we both are free.

BELLS AND WHISTLES

January 29, 1993

I gave you all the bells and whistles. I gave you all the respect and honor you deserved. I would have given you more but there is no more to give.

What do you do when the nearest and dearest person in your life dies? Now one is prepared for death, though some do prepare in a desultory manner.

I went alone to the mortuary. I gave them the pertinent facts, wondered where you should be buried. I don't know. I wended my way back to the way you thought. The way you talked about the men you served with in World War II, the Ordnance Company you served with, attached to the brave and prestigious 82nd Airborne. Your trip to France in a jeep for supplies, your meeting with the English soldiers, your camaraderie with them—all the men you served your country with. You were young, handsome and vital. You were compassionate and brave. You were also both afraid and courageous. You were special, very special. To me you were more than special.

I wanted you to leave this world with all the love I could show you. I arranged a religious service in the small chapel at Golden Gate National Cemetery. The Rabbi spoke the words I had related to him a few days before, about you, a special man, not just another good provider, or husband, but a special man. I requested the Honor Guard. Eight young soldiers fired their guns in the air, taps were blown and I, as your wife, was presented with the American flag for your honorable service to this country.

I put a notice of your death in my hometown paper. You had never lived there, but anyone who would remember me would be assured I remembered you. All that's left now is a marble plaque with your name, rank, date of birth and date of death in a national cemetery along with one hundred twenty-seven thousand other guys who served their country. I gave you a grand send-off. I really did!

THEY ARE COMING BACK

February 1, 1993

I realized last night that my nightmares of a lifetime are coming back. Over the years I've made an accommodation with my bad dreams—my nightly dreams. After my husband died in October 1992, I began slowly to be aware I no longer was having these disturbing dreams. But of course, I was having disturbing days. The dark shadows, the fears and the pain I had been experiencing in my sleep had transferred to my days where I was aware of all the same fears, shadows and much more pain than my nights had been.

Last night I had a nightmare. I pulled myself awake from this terror and then I realized my nightmares are coming back. I think it means the nightmares of my days are diminishing. I can deal with my sleep—I mostly don't remember them and when I do they are short lived. The nightmares of my days these past three months are real, my sorrow is real, my pain is real and the reality is never forgotten. It is a living breathing pain. It goes on and on. Sometimes when I'm talking with people, it goes in the corner and lies down, then as soon as I'm alone, it rises up and joins me.

I hope that since my nightmares are coming back, my days will be less painful, my chest won't feel as tight and slowly, the darkness of my life will go back to the night of dreams.

Since last night, I am hopeful. Maybe I'm beginning to recover from my great loss. Let the nightmares begin.

THE FIRST DAY OF THE REST OF MY LIFE

February 1, 1993

I noticed that today was the first day that I didn't tell anyone my husband had died three months ago. They have all expressed sympathy, but then I hurry past the words and change the subject. Somehow, I have had to acknowledge his presence on the earth. I don't feel sad when I've talked briefly about his demise, but I have the compulsion to insert his recent death into the conversation. I need to cry out, so to speak, and say he was here, he was here. He was such a vital, intelligent man and I did not want him to vanish from this earth so quickly.

Today I went shopping. I talked to at least seven strangers about books (I was in a book store), about linens (I bought a pillow). I bought a calendar. I bought a place mat, and when I came home I realized I had not mentioned his death. I talked about him, but not his death. I am sure the people I chatted with thought he was alive. I talked about a trip to Greece with the Greek woman who works in the book store.

Hey, I don't have to tell anyone else he died. I am sure it will come up now and then, but I guess I'm coming up for air and somewhere deep inside me I, too, will have to welcome the troops back home (I will have to spend the rest of my life with the living.).

You fought the good fight. You lived the good life. I hope to see you someday and if not, I was very, very lucky to have had you so many years.

INSTINCT, INTUITION, BRAINS AND LUCK

February 3, 1993

I am going forward. The going is slow, or seems slow. Actually, the going is in spurts, stops and then the process begins again. There is nothing like having a cold or a mild illness that keeps you confined to your home. You can't go chasing shadows or whatever it is you are doing when you drive to the mall, to the bank, to the grocers and on and on. The chit-chat of casual conversation that keeps your spirits up and then back home to the aloneness, which if you are tired enough, doesn't seem so heavy on your shoulders.

I am going forward. In the quiet time of being alone for a few days, you realize that you have accomplished a lot. You have become your own person. As much as you loved and cared for your mate and as much as you miss him, you can make it.

Sometimes it is relatively easy, chores you have performed all your life are routines. It's the new challenges and believe me, there are challenges which need all the inner strength you can master. You now have to make all decisions alone, you have to take trips alone. You have to eat alone and cook for one. You have no one to really exchange ideas with. Friends can share some of your ideas and are a wonderful part of your new life but the inner you has no real partner.

This new world you have entered is like driving into a new city with no map; no map of the streets, the parks, places of interest. No map. You have to wend your way through this maze and find some point of orientation so that you can find your way through this strange city, country, town. I have always had a good sense of direction. Now I must really put it to good use. I have no idea where I am going, how far or for what purpose. Maybe there is no purpose. I will have to accept what lies ahead. I hope I can find my way.

I'M MY OWN BEST FRIEND

February 3, 1993

When you are an only child, you have to depend on your own resources to survive. Surviving to be defined as how to play alone when it is raining. Surviving to be defined as reading, starting from nursery rhymes, to fairy tales and on up until you reach the books that adults read and can understand. I spent each summer vacation during my childhood years in the Public Library. Being an avid fan of fantasy, I read every book of fairy tales which were on the shelves alphabetically. When I finally reached the last few letters on the alphabet, I begin to feel very sad. I did not know why, but in retrospect I was leaving my fantasy land and emerging to the next stage which I really did not want to enter. I must have gone on reading, though no longer alphabetically. But I read and read and still do.

It has been harder as I've grown older to become as totally absorbed in a book as I did when I was young. The older me had to face the trials and tribulations of life which kept me occupied, and my inner spirit could no longer be submerged in the world of books.

Now I'm an only child again. I use the term "child" metaphorically. I want to try to regain that sense of wonderment and pleasure I derived from reading so long ago. Of course the "child" is still in me and I just have to find it. We never change, not really. We grow up, we grow older but we never really change. I can remember how I felt and the sense of wonderment at the beauty of the world and the excitement of words and ideas that were new to me.

It will take time to reacquaint myself with the "child" within, but if she was my best friend once, she can become my best friend again.

WHAT'S IT ALL ABOUT?

February 4, 1993

People are dying all around us—in every country, town and city. Accidentally, natural causes, suicides, murders, etc. People are dying

We live in this cocoon of life. This haven where death is outside and we turn our backs and only think of death as an inanimate object.

When death invades our personal life (and it will, and it must), we have no idea how to handle it. We can't fight the inanimate, we can't reason with the inanimate and most of all we can't accept the inanimate. How can this joyous life we live end or the lives of those we love actually stop. It is totally unreasonable. I have no answers. Is this all there is? A span of time on earth as a vital, living, bright, creative creature and that's it? It is unacceptable, totally unacceptable! I must make some sense out of the chaos I feel churning inside me. I know the cliché "Time heals"—I really don't believe this. "Time passes," that I believe, "Next year is a year away," that I believe, but the statement that "Time heals" is too simplistic for my taste.

Do I want to heal? My wounds are too deep to be treatable by conventional methods. I don't want to forget my love. I just don't want to have the pain of remembrance. I will just have to wait and see what helps the pain. Maybe "time" will play a part in it or maybe there is another method to be considered. I know the standard ones; keep busy, keep busy. But how busy can you keep? Get a hobby, take a trip, and on it goes. All the advice that has been passed on from one generation to another. I have a feeling that the solution is fairly simple. I just have to make an accommodation with death. Your "death" exists, therefore "you are." I, on the other hand, am "alive," therefore "I am." Someday, I, too, will be in your dimension but for the time being, "I am, I am."

BURNING BRIGHTLY

February 7, 1993

My mind has been lying dormant. The embers were always glowing, but now that I'm alone to explore "the meaning of life," I see small flames emerging from the embers of my inner thoughts. Flames shooting up and I can feel the fire starting to burn in greater intensity.

I never thought about the fire within. I've always had an inner spark that was apparent to anyone who knew me well and maybe, long ago, I knew about the fire that was just below the surface of my consciousness.

I am in awe of this fire that is beginning to take hold of my life. It is frightening in its rapacious desire to be felt and take hold of me. The warmth is almost too intense—it is exciting and threatening. The desire to express all thoughts, feelings, ideas which having fully formed in my brain is debilitating. I feel so tired. I have to learn to control and take charge of the fire within. I will probably make some people uneasy with my exuberance and enthusiasm. It really doesn't matter. Whatever I am is what I will be.

I only hope and wish I can use these newfound fires to do something interesting and gratifying and not let the flames burn themselves out in short bursts. What that will be has not yet made itself known to me.

Ever since I can remember, I have identified with those I've loved. I have used their identity as a crutch to aid me through life. I've been happy enough doing that, but now they are all gone and I have no one but myself to turn to. What I am seeing is burning brightly, but I have to take charge of the self that so cleverly hid from me. How clever am I now? Can I make good use of the "Me" or will the "Me" who I ignored for years take some type of revenge?

I've been told I'm a "strong woman." I am now under pressure, self-imposed, to find out how strong I am. I, alternately, want to hide and go hurriedly out. The recluse, the adventurer. It's fine to be both, but I have to find an outline of sorts and limits to impose on myself. I do not look forward to making these judgments on myself. I realize in many ways I've led a very pampered life emotionally. There was always someone around who thought I was bright, funny, and capable, but the sound is so hollow coming from oneself. I need a sounding board; if not someone else, is just the writing down of these words good enough? I don't think so. It's a beginning and now the search begins.

COMING OUT

February 7, 1993

As I have been talking and meeting new people these last few days, I realize I'm among the disadvantaged minority. I'm a widow now. The word "widow" to me has a very curious sound and the meaning conveys unpleasant comparisons to the black widow spider or to the supposedly "Merry Widow." I hate the word. I hate the sound. "Ow," it hurts.

We are facing a whole new way of living. It is not just living alone part of our lives. It is the way the rest of the world views us. We are to be treated with sympathy, we're included in some couple activities, but very gingerly. It seems the rest of the world really doesn't know how to cope with us. Actually, we're trying hard to cope with ourselves. I find myself talking for both my husband (who is gone) and myself. He was articulate on political affairs, historical events and the media treatment of these. How can I possibly compete with his intellect? I was so proud at the way he could hold his own and convey his ideas on so many subjects in a lucid manner. I, on the other hand, am knowledgeable to an extent on these matters but as he often said, my interest span would wane if I wasn't enthusiastic about something.

I can hold forth on many subjects but which have little social or political bearing on our society. I can engage in small talk (which he detested) and find pleasure in triviality when it arises.

I find I am coming out of the closet at this point in my life. I've been in a twosome relationship most of my life and have found great comfort in it. As a single, this totally new experience is dramatic and stressful. I am coming into a new period of my life alone and will be judged solely on my assets. I no longer have the protective wall of a man who stands between me and them. It's just me. I have to be careful and not reveal myself too quickly. I have to really know more about the me. I'm bright enough, I'm cheerful. Should I be more thoughtful sounding? I know I can't act sad and forlorn. That part of me is strictly private. I will have to hone my image as carefully as possible so that I won't intimidate the outside world with my "strong" woman image. "Strong is a good word but I have to soften the strong. Underneath, I'm just as vulnerable as the next person and probably not very different from all the others of this new group "the minority of ones."

Up to the present, it has been a learning experience. I have learned quite a lot about myself, but I have a long way to go.

SHE, WHO WALKS ALONE

February 11, 1993

I'm not shutting down. I'm not shutting off. I think I have to lay low for awhile and regenerate myself. I've met new people, went to new places, ate in new restaurants and rediscovered the world. I've been away too long. I think I have to re-think my priorities. I will still keep meeting new people, going to new places, but I have to change my pace. I just might, in this new burst of energy and awareness, miss something of value, which will be beneficial to me, not monetarily or even spiritually. I don't want to miss it. I don't want to run too fast. Life is to be savored, not devoured.

I've just started to put the brakes on and I'm still moving a little too fast for comfort, but as I begin coasting, I will begin to relax. And as the old saying goes, "smell the flowers."

Life is sweet and so very precious. Death is so final. Each of us in our own way will experience so many emotions in our lifetime. I sometimes feel that I have experienced too many and not enough.

This will be my time in the future to set my life in order—to do, to say, act out of my most inner feelings. I have begun this process but I've only started in a random fashion. I want to make sense out of all of this, or nonsense as the case may be.

I am tired, but not too tired. I care deeply about so many people, but not to the extent that I am absorbed into another person's life. I am an independent entity who needs and wants the world around me but it is of vital importance that "I stand alone." I have never "stood alone." It's a new step for me—sometimes I'm shaky. When you stand alone, there is no one to lean on, so like a baby, I have to learn to walk and keep my balance. I'm a quick learner and if I feel like I'm falling, I'll remember my mother's words, "You can do anything you want to do," and my husband's words, "You're the smartest woman I've ever known." Words to live by. I can't disappoint either one of them. They had complete trust in my ability. I hope they were right. I refuse to prove them wrong.

"She, who goes with the flow."

STARTING TO WRITE

Friday, February 12, 1993

I've just read the first chapter of a book, "Writing Down the Bones." It says write down what you think at this moment. At this moment, it seems that I could have written the first chapter. I do write with a fast pen because I'm writing emotional thoughts. I don't plan what I'm going to write; I don't even know I'm going to write until I sit down and thoughts come rushing at me. I feel like I'm in a crowded bus. I'm crushed by thoughts, bits and pieces, words and phrases. I have had a crowd in my brain all my life and now I'm letting them emerge; all shapes, sizes, colors, sense and nonsense. I don't feel happy by their emergence. Actually, I don't really know them very well. They are like my neighbors who have lived on my street for years and, yet, I have no idea what they are all about or if I want to know them.

I've always had a tremendous desire to live and I use the word "live" loosely. I know I'm alive, but to live is something entirely different. I want to squeeze the juice of the orange of life. I mustn't be impatient. I will take a deep breath and be patient. I don't think patience is a virtue, but in my case it just might be a necessity.

THE LONELY VALENTINE

February 14, 1993

Happy Valentine's Day! Oh yes, happy—my heart is laying in the ground in a national cemetery. I never thought about the future without my heart. It is an empty feeling in that cavity of my body where my heart is supposed to be. A dull ache which is constantly with me. Sometimes when I'm busy talking and visiting with people, I forget I have this pain. It always returns though, it really never leaves me. It's awfully hard to live without a heart.

For so many years, my heart lived a full life. It loved, it cared, it worried, it agonized, all for my husband and then he died. Possibly someday it will return to my body. The heart has so many functions that go beyond the primary one "to keep you alive." It needs to love, to care, to worry, and to agonize. I guess I don't really need my heart right now. I suppose if the need ever arises, it will return and if there is no need it will stay buried next to the remains of the heart that was its mate.

What does a heartless person do? How do you live? You pretend to care, you pretend to love, you pretend to worry. I think I am still capable of all the above emotions, maybe I'm not. I don't have a broken heart that can be fixed. My heart is gone. I guess you can live without a heart, but there is very little pleasure in the living; it's just existing.

My ears are muffled against the sounds of life as I once knew it. All my senses are diminished. I am looking at the world through a dusty, unclear window. It is still a beautiful world and there are still kind, loving people inhabiting it. But, I am not a part of this world. I am alone with no heart. I am alone.

EASY DOES IT

February 15, 1993

I'm cutting back on my intake. It is time to savor all the new things that have entered my life. Ever since I've been alone, I have embraced so many new friendships. Some will endure and others will be short lived. I want to keep spreading my wings and fly back and forth and talk to, be with, share with everyone I meet.

I began to realize I've spread myself too thin and I won't be able to concentrate on the people I've met with whom I share the most common interest. I've been very lucky. I've met probably the most interesting people in my life these past few months. In the past there were others, but I could never pursue a total commitment to anyone for any length of time.

I was already totally committed. Now I am alone. There is so much more of me to share—this sharing I treasure, but I have to cut back and reduce my calorie count of people. I want to be able to enjoy my new life and don't want it overburdened by additional weight.

It is strange that I have moved so quickly from wife to "*swinging*" single. My *swinging* entails very little movement, just a gentle pushing (which I am doing to get myself started) and talking and listening, all of which is stimulating and reassuring that I am becoming my own person. I can make it alone.

I have something to say.

The time has come, at least for now, to limit my comings and goings. I want to enjoy the now that I have created. I want to enjoy the new friends I have made. I don't want to go off the deep end and go "bungy jumping" into an emotional abyss. Life is becoming too sweet to miss out on the flavorful friends I have made. I don't want to stuff myself out of panic. I still feel pangs of panic, but I'm beginning to gain control. Good for you, kid! You're going to make it!

WEEDS

February 20, 1993

I'm wandering through the widow weeds. I just realized the meaning of the expression "widow's weeds." I'm sure if I look it up in the dictionary, it will have no relation to the interpretation I am putting on it. Perhaps it will, but I will look it up later so as not to close my mind against my definition. For a little over four months, I have been a widow. From the beginning until now, I have gone through a gamut of emotions. I am not progressing from sad to happier. I am going around in circles. When I'm out and doing, I mostly forget the deep pain I feel when I'm alone. When I'm alone I sometimes forget the pain and talk to the one that is gone. I have no idea if he can hear me but it's what I would say to him if he were here. Things about money, about people, about purchases, about traveling, about my clothes, my food, about our cat, about my fears and most of all I tell him I'm okay, or almost okay.

I suppose I'm doing this to reassure myself. Other people can tell me I am doing fine and that "time heals," etc.—but I know that I'll have to do it myself—heal myself. Bandage my own inner wounds ("so with a little help from your presence which still permeates our house, I'm trying to heal").

I am among the weeds. They are tall and thick. I am wandering among the weeds. I see a glimmer of sun and then the shadows close around me. I am in a maze of weeds. I find it's better at times to try to push myself into a clearing, but the weeds are still blocking my view. Sometimes it is better to resign myself to the comforting fronds of the weeds as they enclose me.

I've looked it up in the dictionary; black, mourning dress or veil customarily worn by the widows. It is so much more than that. It is a state of being. I can feel the suffocation of being trapped within these weeds. At times I can sometimes feel the blades against my skin as I push through them. But mostly, it is the lack of air and the seemingly endless jungle of weeds that annoys me. The word "annoy" doesn't even begin to define how I feel. I guess it's a combination of annoyance, fear, frustration, and denial that I feel.

It is so difficult to breathe at times. My chest is tight and I turn my head away and try to concentrate on something else; the newspaper, TV, a phone call to a friend, and as a last resort, I get in the car and drive. Drive out of the weeds, out, out. I hope I can leave them behind soon. It will never be soon enough.

I think I can begin a new life without too many aches and pains of my recent past life. I do not know. I don't want to go in circles for the rest of my life. I don't want to end without loving or caring again but I am resigned to the fact that if I can find the exit from my widow weeds—there is a possibility I will have a new life of sorts.

AN AUTHOR IN SEARCH

February 23, 1993

Early in the waking hours, my mind kept stirring and I gave up sleep and went into my reminiscing mode. My life has changed, drastically changed. I am alone, totally alone for the first time in my life. Of course, there are appendages; cousins, friends and acquaintances, but no one close, really close.

My home is a source of comfort and healing and then I came to the realization that I am not alone. They are all around me; they are the pictures I have all through my house. My husband, the two of us together, my mother and father in separate frames and together. My mother and father and my brother. My husband's grandfather, grandmother and his assorted aunts and uncles; his mother when she was very small. They are all gone. They are dead; some recent, and some long ago, but they are all here.

I want to put them in perspective. I remember Pirandello's play "Six Characters in Search of an Author." The tables have turned. I, "the Author," am in search. The leading man is my husband. Who else could play this important role but a strong, virile, intelligent, handsome man. My parents will play parents, a role they played in life. My mother, the gentle, intuitive, warm and loving person she was in life. My father, the sensitive, intelligent man who lived with despair. My brother, the unusual boy so gifted who died so young, his potential never realized. My husband's grandfather, who died before my husband was born; the tall, elegant man who came to America with great hopes for the future who died too soon from working in the sweatshops of New York. His grandmother, who survived and remained an independent woman who gave more love to her grandchildren than she received in return. My husband loved her unconditionally until the day he died. My husband's mother would make the seventh character and since she was the seventh child, I think that would be appropriate.

Now that I, "the Author," have seven characters and I have assigned each their role, they continue to play them out for me. The leading man is in every scene. The parents are very important as they impart their own lines to the play. The grandparents have a smaller role. They have been gone so long that it is difficult to write many lines for them. However, they are also integral to the play. His mother goes in and out of the scenes. She's a vivid presence, but not endearing. There is something missing in her character. Maybe six would have been enough, but she is a part of the play nonetheless.

My search is beginning to materialize. I have the characters. I know some of them well. I know some of their reactions. I would probably be surprised by their inner thoughts. I would like to become more familiarized with their unrealized dreams, their unresolved conflicts. They belong to me.

A good author can bring his characters to life. Of course, it is only on paper; but the paper has a life. It can breathe; and anyone who can read and feel the energy of these people who once lived and who did all the ordinary things, but who were unique in their own special way and who will not come this way again. They deserve the life I am trying to give them. If anyone can sense what I feel about my characters, I will have succeeded in keeping them alive.

No one lives forever, but poems, books and plays—some live on for centuries. I'm not bold enough to think I can give myself or them an endless life, but if they stay with me until I join them, that will be good enough. It will really be good enough.

LIMITED PARTNERSHIP

February 27, 1993

We had a limited partnership. It was limited by life. The time, the amount of money invested, the emotional ups and downs were all part of this partnership. We even signed a contract, a contract of Marriage, which I adhered to. "In sickness and in health, until death do us part."

You did your part to perform the duties outlined in this contract; actually you went beyond and performed beyond the duties required. You gave all of yourself—I think sometimes, too much. It was your way, all or nothing. There were the "nothing" times but they were insignificant compared to your "all." I, on the other hand, tried very hard to stay in the middle ground. I did not want to be consumed by resentment if I went overboard and did not feel adequately rewarded. But I always gave as much as possible, not only because I cared, but it was my way.

As in all limited partnerships, this one came to an end. I am feeling the despair of bankruptcy, not of financial loss, but emotional loss. How very strange it is to find oneself as the only living partner. How do I keep the business of living a viable entity now that I have total control of all the problems that will and must arise? How do I make the right decisions with no sounding board—no partner? Will I be able to keep running in place or will I fall backwards and drift? I want to use your strength and knowledge that you have imparted to me. I want to find contentment in my future, but I desperately do not want to fail. I have no fear of failure. I just want to make you proud of me. You often told me "I was the smartest woman you ever knew," and I want to live up to those words no matter what endeavor I choose. It will be interesting to see if you were right.

ETERNAL STANDARD TIME

March 4, 1993

The phone rang last night in the small hours of the morning, approximately three o'clock a.m. I have an answering machine that rings twice and then answers. I keep it on most of the time. The phone rang two times precisely and stopped. It rang again about five minutes later, two times exactly and stopped. Wrong number? No. They would ring longer. Was it you? I'm here wanting to talk to you. I'm on Pacific Standard time, don't you know? Maybe not, you are on Eternal Standard time and since you can't reach me, and your voice can't be recorded, I am left with this empty feeling of no one to talk to. The rest of the world is busy and no one cares for me like you did.

I feel I've been thrown into a jungle. I feel all the strange animals about me. Some friendly, some indifferent, some are deadly and ferocious, and I am glad I have a cave to hide in. I want to venture out and feel free and safe as I did when you were with me, but oh, it's different now.

I'm just beginning to realize the difference. I am going to have to build a shield to protect me against the wild winds that are blowing filled with greed, jealousy, and cruelty. Will I be able to survive this world or remain a recluse and wait until I enter yours? If my time here was short, I would choose the latter. But since I do not know my destiny, I will probably keep trying to push out and then retrench to fight another day.

If I am lucky, eventually I will be able to cope better. I hate the world without you. It's mostly mean and cold. Did you try to call me last night to warn me and console me? I'm inconsolable now. I need you now and I needed you all my life. Can I make it without you? Will there ever be more than surface joy? I don't know.

Tonight, I am pessimistic. Call me again. I don't care what means of communication you use. I'll be waiting.

IT'S THE PITS

March 5, 1993

As I awakened early, very early, I felt I was walking around the pit of despair. I have been doing a balancing act on the edge, and I seem to be about to fall. I regain my composure and move away from the pit only to be brought inexorably back to the darkness that seems to be beckoning to me. It looks inviting, this darkness, this black hole. I would like nothing better than to be consumed by whatever lies in the pit, but I am afraid, so afraid that within that darkness further terrors may be waiting. I can only go forth each day into the light and not think about the pit of despair which I must confront from time to time. At times I forget about the sadness within me that almost drives me mad.

I must move away from anything and anyone that causes me to agonize. Agonizing comes in many forms: anger, rejection, indifference, all that causes me to agonize. I need the positive, the good, the caring, the joy, the flexible around me. No pressures, no pettiness. I have to learn to be a stranger and resist the urge for companionship in exchange for being treated in my view less compassionately, than I treat others.

I would hope I would have the courage to respond to what I feel are insults. I no longer have a knight in shining armor to come to my rescue, so I will take up the sword and fight my own fights. Only courage has kept me among other things from falling in the pit. I need courage to take charge of my life and not resort to "feeling sorry for myself."

It's too bad we have to fight. It's too bad that not enough people are kind and gentle and compassionate. They are not. It's a fact of life. So arm yourself not for the offense, but for the defense. I am using my pen for my sword, it is my Excalibur!

ALL SHOOK UP

March 5, 1993

Who is rattling my cage? I'm being shaken up pretty good. I guess we're all in a cage of sorts, but you don't realize you're surrounded by bars until the shaking begins. I don't see anyone. I only feel myself being tossed about. I hurry back to my own habitat. At least I won't be a casualty laying on the street if the doors of my cage open. At least here I'll only end up on the floor and be able to pick myself up.

Who is rattling my cage? Why am I in here? How can I co-exist with this now imaginary cage existence, and will I be able to safely exist this heaving, unstable motion which permeates my being?

Okay. You know why you're all shook up? You just don't know how to handle it. There is no handling, of course. You just have to let "it" run its course and you have no choice but to run with it. How long can you run? Another rhetorical question: "How high is up?"

SOMETHING OLD, SOMETHING NEW

March 6, 1993

I went out to look at furniture this morning (a sofa to be exact). I want to change the couch in my den. It doesn't go with the rug, it's too soft, it's too big for the room. All of the above.

As I was driving near my house, I passed a sign—"Estate Sale." Normally I don't peruse these type of shopping areas. My husband always felt depressed looking at other people's possessions. People who had died or been retired to a nursing home or some other end zone.

I went in. The place was swarming with people, picking up and putting down everything that whoever had lived here had purchased so long ago. By the looks of most things, it was long ago. Everything look well loved. I sat on the couch in the living room and talked to a delightful child with big brown eyes. He was one of the cashiers. His grandmother ran the Estate Sale, his mother was the other cashier. But John, age eight (I asked him), told me he didn't need a calculator, he was good in math and he was handling the "customers" very efficiently. I sat near his station (chair and table) and we talked.

The longer I sat on the couch, the more I realized that I would like to own it. It needed recovering, but it had an elegance that I remembered from another time. It felt just right. We seemed to meld together, this old well-loved couch and this well-loved woman. I made an offer. Estate sales seem to be handled like auctions. The matriarch just called me. Grandmother of estate sales, she said, "You bought yourself a couch."

I said, "Fine."

She will be by soon to pick up my check. My upholsterer has been called. He will pick it up. He will recover it. I will have this charming formal sofa enter my life as "something old and something new." Part of the wedding tradition has been reestablished in my life. How odd that today, I'm reliving part of my marriage. Obviously, we two were meant for each other.

I HEAR THE GENTLE VOICES CALLING

March 8, 1993

"I'm coming, I'm coming, for my head is bending low, I hear the gentle voices calling." A few lines from a song. My head is filled with songs, melodies I haven't heard for years. Words unremembered are all enveloping me. A warm evening, a few nights ago, I found myself humming and singing to myself. Songs from the nineteen forties or nineteen fifties and some from way back, to songs I learned in elementary school. Why the regression into music?

The songs are like old friends who I haven't seen in years and we are partaking in the joy of sound. The banality of the usual lyrics (love, longing, laughter and loss) do not sound banal to me now. They are very meaningful. They remind me to remember people associated with the words and music. I find myself smiling and at other times I feel the pain in my heart.

Mostly, it is a reverie. It's a place to go in your mind. A time that has no boundaries and a comfort that has no hand to hold, but nevertheless the pleasure of remembrance is very real. I would stay in this world forever, but I know I am just passing through. I have moved through many passages, I would stay a little longer. Here is where the heart is. When I move off in whatever direction my destiny takes me, I would wish to take no excess baggage, but I would oh-so-wish to take my heart.

DEAR, DEPARTED AND BELOVED

March 8, 1993

How I hate those words, how I hate those words! Each one unto themselves are okay. "Dear," how dear! Departed, "where did you go?." "Beloved," of course.

Why the litany? When did it become part of the funeral ritual? Every now and then these words run through my consciousness and I get mad. Now, why am I mad? Can I not accept your departure? True, I can't accept it, but why do these three words make me so angry? Am I only seeing "departed"? And the word "beloved" is too formal.

Of course, you are dear, departed and beloved. So what? Is that all you are or were? What do I expect from rituals performed by well-meaning people who never knew the "departed"? They are just doing their job. Someday, the rituals should be re-written so that the surviving member will only remember words like "It's been nice to know you," or "I'll be seeing you." It seems I'm back to my songs, but they actually hit the nail on the head of most emotions sooner or later.

I guess there should be no words at a funeral, only music and let each person attending find their personal memory or a tribute to the "dear, departed and beloved."

I'm trying to think of the right song for you. There are so many that could apply. I suppose the one that is most suitable is that old song, "The Man I'll Love." I'd change words, of course, from "Someday he'll come along," to "The day he came along," and of course, "I'll never let him go," will have to be changed to "I'll have to let him go."

"Dear, Departed and Beloved." I'll have to let you go.

THE NEST EGG

March 9, 1993

How can you throw away a lifetime with someone? You can't. You just have to live off the residuals. We invested totally in our marriage. We shared almost everything. Of course, we shared our home, our food, our trips, our friends, and other assorted material items. It is the intangible we shared that is most difficult to replace; actually it's irreplaceable.

I know how you thought about most people, politics, pleasures and daily events that came up. I can almost hear your response to a question in my mind relating to "should I? I consult you every day, sometimes out loud. Sometimes silently, and await your wise and compassionate answers. Sometimes, I disagree and then mull it over and discuss it with you again until I arrive at a more rational solution.

These are my residuals of my years spent with you. You are gone, but I still have all your wisdom and wit, somehow stored in my memory bank. You have left me your strength. I need it now and am using it—I think wisely. You have left me your decision making and I'm going forward in making them alone now. You left me your compassion and I'm trying to be selective and be wise enough to not throw it around in a frenzy of loneliness and a desire to be liked.

Most of all, you have left me your intelligence. I'll never acquire your level, but I will try very hard to analyze my behavior, so that you will be proud of me. I wish I were able to grasp the essence of you and hold it close to me, but it eludes me. I can feel it, I can sense it, but I can't touch it. You were here and now you are gone. Of course, you are not altogether gone, as long as I have these residuals in my account. And oddly enough, they are collecting interest.

By my own doing, whatever I'm doing, I'm building up my investment in life. I would hope someday to be as rich as I was when you were here. We were truly wealthy. We had a wealth of love, we had a wealth of total commitment to each other. I never realized how truly rich we were. Of course, we had debits, disagreements and frustrations. The total sum, however, was far higher than either of us imagined. Thank heavens, you left me this nest egg of residuals so that I have something to build on. I am building. The blueprint is not complete, but the planning has begun. It should be interesting to see the finished product.

WE NEVER HAD PARIS

March 9, 1993

I went out to the cemetery today. I put fresh flowers on your grave and rearranged the two small American flags I had placed there last week. The wind had blown one down. I looked down at the marble plaque: your name, your rank, your branch of service, your birth date and your death date. Above all this, was the Star of David. I find it so hard to believe that all of you that remains is a marble marker in a military cemetery surrounded by over one hundred twenty-seven thousand men who fought in wars and served their country.

I kept hearing the words from the movie "Casablanca." Humphrey Bogart telling Ingrid Bergman when she is about to leave him forever, "We'll always have Paris."

All day long I keep saying that we'll have—what? We'll always have, but what is it we'll really always have? We'll never always have each other again. We'll never have another day together or another meal together. What will we always have? I have memories, but the elusive magic moment that I am trying to remember evades me. What will we always have? I try to think back. There were many magic moments, many sad moments. There were months, years of moments, but what was the most special one? Was it our wedding day? Was it when we bought a house? Was it one of our trips? Was it when you were with me in the hospital when I was near death?

No. Those were all important and meaningful, but those aren't the one. Maybe there is no one, maybe because there were so many highlights in our marriage and our life together that I can't become dramatic and take a line in a movie that narrows love down to one place at one time. There were too many places and too many times. We always had many, many moments in our many years together. You always had me, and still do, and I'll have you... always, always.

LEAN ON ME

March 10, 1993

I keep remembering and remembering; and what really stands out is your strength, your ability to take charge, to protect. When I lovingly called you my "hero," it was not in jest—you were truly my hero. You stood between me and the world. You were the wall I could lean on, you were the guard at the gate. You kept the "values of life" at bay. Yet you were a gentle man. A man who loved to be touched and stroked, a man who was pleased by small kindnesses, a man no one knew but me. A very private man who never truly believed in himself. A mind so keen and vision so wide and yet missed seeing itself.

I saw you, maybe not the whole of you. I spent hours trying to fathom the parts of you I could not reach. It doesn't matter now. I'm left alone but you left me much of your strength and wisdom. That is truly my inheritance and I must use it well.

SOLITARY CONFINEMENT

March 10, 1993

The condemned ate a hearty meal. I awakened this morning, I realized how alone I was. No one to say, "Good morning," no one to say, "What will we have for breakfast?" or, "What are your plans for today?"

There is no one, not a living, breathing person inhabiting my space. If it was not for my cat, Finian, who fortunately makes his presence known (when he is hungry), my only contact with the human race is by phone or opening my doors to leave and meet someone or to welcome someone.

I am living in solitary confinement. My cell is large, actually a whole house, which gives me the freedom to move around, but my heart is living in a small cell. Is this going to be the rest of my life? Am I only going to share at measured times with measured people? I cannot foresee my future. It is possible I will make an accommodation with loneliness. Many people do. I have been lonely in my life; even a shared life does not preclude one from being lonely.

I was an only child from the age of ten. I learned early to play alone much of the time, to read, to use my imagination and have imaginary companions. As I grew older, there were other priorities to keep loneliness at bay. Of course, I had my parents, especially my mother to talk to whenever I needed to talk. There were friends, but those times did not fill the day. Looking back, I was born so full of life that I was bursting at the seams. I played and laughed and never seemed to stop long enough to let loneliness get a grip on me. I am still full of life, but I can't seem to run away from loneliness as fast as I once did. It's hovering around the corners and I see it taking shape as I move quickly into another frame of mind. Perhaps it's time to confront it. Perhaps it's time to end the battle with loneliness. Maybe its not the monster I expect.

Enter—loneliness, welcome—loneliness. What do you want of me? Are you enemy or friend? Perhaps you are whatever I want you to be. Perhaps you are that quiet time I need to gather my thoughts and sort out my life. Perhaps you are that time for the rest I need, instead of chasing shadows. Perhaps you are my friend and I can use you to think and come to terms with, and to utilize my energies for positive ideas. It's hard to quit running away from you. I have to put the brakes on. You could be the good in my life from now on. Meanwhile, I am still living in solitary confinement.

THE PROMISE

March 10, 1993

He said, "Stay, stay," and I stayed.

He was dying. I held his hand. I held his arm. I touched him. I stroked him. I bent over his bed and stayed. I stayed for hours. I would have stayed for days if he could have stayed with me. He fell into a deep sleep after they gave him enough drugs to take away his pain. I called his name. He was leaving me. I stayed.

Earlier in the day, he asked, "Have you eaten?" I assured him I had.

He then said, "Come to bed."

I said, "There is not enough room. The bed you are in now is too small for the both of us. When you come home, we'll be in our big bed." He said very little.

I had brought him root beer earlier. He had not been allowed any food or drink for days. It was all intravenous feeding. He sipped a little (his favorite drink). I felt completely helpless in the face of my husband's dying. I could not cry enough. I could not drown myself in tears. I could only hold his hand and stroke his arm and forehead. In the silence, I watched him leaving. In my mind, I was saying over and over, "Don't leave, don't leave!"

But he did and now I am "staying" alone. I am so alone without the most important part of me gone. The most important part of me is dust beneath a marble slab in a national cemetery. Oh, how I wish I was with you. Oh, how I wish we were dust together. We will be, someday. But I wish it were now or soon. I am only living dust. A wind could blow me away; a broom could sweep me out the door, but the body that surrounds the dust is not so easily moved. I'm like a large doorstop sitting on my dust.

He had told me a day or two before "I'm dying, I'm dying."

Then the tears did stream down my face. All I remembered saying was, "We'll be together, whatever happens, we'll be together." That is a promise I will keep. Someday we will be together, that I promise!

NUMBER, PLEASE

March 11, 1993

How do you describe a "flat spot in the road"? I know what I mean, but I can't define it in relation to human emotions. It is like a part of a tape that doesn't record your voice or when you program your VCR. You come upon a blank area that did not record the show. On the phone, I guess it would be when you are disconnected accidentally.

I have a lot of flat spots or unrecorded moments or disconnected thoughts. I'm rolling along through the day, whether by car, by foot, or sitting doing trivial things and I hit this blank spot. I guess I'm disconnected for whatever period of time it takes to get back on track. I have reached a number which is no longer in service. I can try again. I have to wait until the lines are clear and try again. Does everyone have flat spots in their road? I suppose so, but they are probably too busy or involved to notice and just go over them.

At the moment, I can't go over, around or through them. I have to wait. Mostly it seems I go through them, but it is hard. It's like walking through a thick fog or perhaps a blinding snow storm. You cannot see where you are going but something is pushing or pulling you. Much of the time, I would just rather wait and try not to move through this impasse, but I guess there's too much life left in me to give up.

I'll try the number again, Operator. Maybe I misdialed.

TODAY

March 11, 1993

A typical day. I don't sleep well. Last night was a bummer. I finally got up around one-thirty a.m. and watched television for an hour (a stupid program). Oh, "sleep that knits up the ravell'd sleave of care," Macbeth, Act II. Finally a few hours and the calling of my cat around seven-thirty a.m., it doesn't matter. I've been waking and looking at the clock hourly.

Breakfast, big deal. Cat eats well. I eat well enough. I try to read the paper; full of blood and guts and riots and politics. What should be done? Can it be done and why has it not been done before now? The repetition of the news is not only tiring, it's boring.

Called my lawyer. What about my papers? Changing title of house? Making a new will? No grand malpractice suit? No slip and fall accident case? Just a few papers. He says he'll call me back. So far, six hours later, no call. Carolyn called and talked; great gal. Called Daria; asked about her mother who had cataract surgery and gave her brief greetings and request she call. She did.

Okay. Should take down comforter to Laundromat. All the down from the top has moved to the bottom. Ha! "Down moved down." Was told to put in large dryer; down would move. Man in Laundromat said "I don't think so, take it to the cleaners." Honest proprietors said "Down won't move, even if cleaned. Maybe try a large dryer in Laundromat, if it works okay. If not, at least you won't waste money on cleaning.

Went to Laundromat near cleaners. Put in twenty-five cents. Comforter is nice and warm, but down very stubborn and refuse to move. Go to pick up old typewriter I bought and took to be cleaned. Very heavy, though small and portable. Maybe over forty years old. Picked up—don't think typewriter store did anything but change ribbons. Oh well, so what. Everybody isn't honest. Most people cheat. Some little cheat, some big cheat.

Went to grocery store. Bought asparagus and package of small rice cakes on sale. They are good and happy snacks. Also buttermilk. Maybe I'll make Irish soda bread in bread machine. I think it needs buttermilk.

Home. Take sheets out of washer; put in dryer. Make bed. Eat corn flakes and milk (watch flakes float). It's almost three o'clock. Typical day not yet over. There's cat to feed again, myself to feed again. Maybe phone calls to make and receive. Television to watch later or maybe I'll tape it. Tonight I'll sleep, I hope I'll sleep.

Tomorrow will be another typical day, but different typical. I'm invited to new friends. Should be interesting. I've bought small presents for new friends. Yesterday was typical day, too. Met two new people, but don't want to talk about them now. My God, is this all there is or is all there was?

SALUTE REX

March 12, 1993

I never knew Rex. I never saw Rex. I never even saw a picture of Rex. Rex was my husband's first love, his dog from approximately age ten to age twenty. Rex was half German Shepherd and half Husky. My husband had been bitten by a rabid dog when he was very young, five or six. He had to have the series of shots against rabies which were very painful and left him with an overwhelming fear of dogs. When he saw a dog after that, he would turn back and walk around the block to avoid any contact. Some wise person, maybe a doctor, suggested the only way to get over this phobia, which was consuming him, was to get a puppy.

Into the picture came Rex; a furry, loving creature that immediately became one of the early loves of his life. Rex, the friend who ran around the lake with him in his early years. Sometimes even Rex tired. It's pretty hard to keep up with an active determined runner of fourteen or fifteen years old.

Rex, the hero. Once he had attained his growth, he was a large handsome guy. He began to prove himself beyond the call of duty. Once a child walked into the street, a neighbor's child, unwittingly walking into the street, Rex was on alert. He ran and pulled the child by his clothes to the curb, out of danger. The maid that worked in the house saw it and told all who would listen about this remarkable dog.

My husband's father was involved in union affairs and in those times and those days, violent means were used to stem the tide of unionism. An ambush was awaiting his father one evening. Food for Rex had been placed in a likely spot spiked with poison. Rex ate the food, but fortunately being a strong dog, his stomach rebelled and the food was discharged. Rex, now again became aware of danger, tracked the ambushers and drove them away. He had a piece of clothing in his mouth. He even got accolades from my husband's father who had never paid much attention to Rex.

Oh, Rex, you were a vital part of a young man growing up. You gave love unselfishly, loyalty willingly and you taught a young man these traits. My husband might have been the loving, courageous man he was without a Rex, but I'm sure this dog solidified his personality to a greater degree. I wish I had a picture of Rex. He said he had these large warm eyes and you could look into his face and see him thinking. Thinking "what can I do to please him"? And I am thinking what can I do to please both of them. I salute you both, you were the good, the brave, and the loyal. I salute you.

MY BRIGADOON

March 12, 1993

Brigadoon is a story about a magical place that comes to life every hundred years. For twenty-four hours, the people who inhabit Brigadoon live this one special day, which is filled with laughter, dance, sunshine and love. One day... One glorious day which will be repeated in another century.

I have lived for many years in my Brigadoon. As I look out at the sky, the city, the beauty is breathtaking. I feel I have lived each day to the brim, but now I am falling between the cracks.

Falling into despair, falling into a land of memories. My Brigadoon, my beautiful life, has changed forever. Yet, it was magical and I have days and days to remember.

GETTING DOWN TO BRASS TACKS

March 12, 1993

I'm becoming concerned with practical realities. It just dawned on me that in the midst of the flotsam and jetsam of my daily life. I am dealing with the ordinary; the buying of items, the returning of unused and unsuitable items. I've been making calls relating to money, maintenance of my home, fixing of my car, getting new glasses, getting a couch recovered, and getting information.

I only realized today that I'm getting down to brass tacks and have been; but never put a tag that said "brass tacks" on any of my daily moves. I've felt I've been moving through a haze (a clear haze), but that my vision is impaired. Of course, it is. No one can go through a death of one's mate without encountering a distorted view of life.

Apparently, I've been dealing with essentials out of habit. I have become a rather good card player. A new hand has been dealt to me and I am playing to my strong suit. I don't even know how to play cards in the common usage of the game, but I seem to be winning, at least in some games. I'm not a gambler, so I hold my hand close to my vest, so to speak. But I am playing my cards very well for an amateur.

The game is "Reality," and I must have a talent for it; not an expert, not a trophy contestant, just another adequate participant in the game of life. How about this? I've been dealt a new hand and I seem to be holding my own. As they used to say and I don't know who "they" were, "Good on Me!."

BALLS OF FIRE

March 12, 1993

I am growing cajones. Now that the master is gone, gone to greener pastures, I have to assume his role to some degree. He was a take-charge man, a "you-can't-push-me-around" kind of guy. No bullshit, he was totally fair and totally honest, but never walked away from a fight.

Now I'm in charge. It's not easy. The world is tough. You have to tough it out, or at least try to stay even or you're ground under its heels. I've never had to fight the fight. I had my warrior husband who never had to pick up a weapon. He was the weapon. His essence, his strength, his intelligence, his ability to articulate, his grace under pressure and, when all else failed, he blew, like a volcano, he blew; ashes and dust and debris would come tumbling down on his opponents. He was usually the winner, but not always. Certain emotional battles were never won. He couldn't fight his innate gentleness. When others too vulnerable were involved, he stepped away.

Now I'm in charge. The woman warrior is emerging. I have to be tougher, stronger than I've ever been in my life. "The King is dead. Long live the Queen." Being in charge and taking a hard line gives you a rush which can leave you exhausted, but exhilarated. I'm beginning to have an inkling of what it is like to have "cajones." I use the word because in English it is vulgar; but in Spanish, its use can mean "strong," "guts," or "integrity."

It is a challenge to confront people, especially in the service industry to "Do the right thing." I don't want to become a "tough cookie," a "hard case." I want to stay a woman, but if it takes a little bit away from my femininity, so be it. Damn, "the King" would be proud of me! I can almost hear him saying, "Don't let them push you around," "Don't be a wimp." "When you're right, stand up for yourself, don't be a man; be yourself." Between you and me though, the "Cajones" are a big help.

WHO AM I?

March 13, 1993

It's show time. Each day I go into my act. Sometimes it's a repeat of an act I've honed to a fine art; not original, but if I have a new audience, it won't be old to them. I have many personas, all happy, cheerful, intelligent, but I have yet to create the character that I feel comfortable with.

As I venture on the stage of life, I immediately greet whoever I encounter with a smile. This is my warm-up act. I'm not a comedian. I am this friendly, open, seemingly naive and trusting soul. It's a good opening act. I put the audience at ease.

Act I—Talk, interact with others, keep it light, don't be dramatic. Drama doesn't seem to be my cup of tea. Be concerned about others' problems, but not to the extent you share tears, just warm words of friendship. Give no advice, if possible.

Act II—Now my character is more relaxed in surroundings. Shows more interest in others but still is unsure how the role should be handled. I would like to feel at home in this character, but the essence evades me. Who is she? What does she really think? What does she really feel? I will have to let more time pass before I can truly define my role in this play. There is an Act III, but I haven't read it or perhaps it hasn't been written. I don't know how the play ends, but all plays end. I hope that eventually my character will be able to know her lines and give a sterling performance. She has potential, but the results are not in yet.

BEYOND THE THRESHOLD

March 13, 1993

Have you ever had this strange feeling: your jaws seem to tighten, an overpowering aura seems to encase you. It's terrifying in its total immersement. You seem trapped in some sort of giant vise. I can talk on the phone and laugh and be animated and all seems well. There is just the conversation, the exchange of thoughts and you are content. Then you hang up. No more voices, no more sounds; just the emptiness, total emptiness. You try to keep busy, but how busy can you keep?

You go out. You drive somewhere, anywhere. You look at things, brief conversations with strangers, but sooner or later you have to return to your point of origin. For a few minutes, you are okay, but eventually you put your purchases away and do this or that and sit down. You again enter this, all I can think of to describe it is, "the dead zone."

There is truly no life in your space. You know you are breathing, but you feel like you are choking. Pick up the phone, talk to someone, hear a voice, any voice. The need is so painful that you fight against it. Read a book, turn on the television. Anything. Leave the dead zone. Sometimes it works. Mostly, it doesn't. You just have to learn to live here and hope that eventually the temperature within the zone will change. More oxygen, perhaps, to help you breathe again. A lessening of the pressure against your temples; an objective to hopefully be attained.

How long will I have to live in the dead zone? Months, years, forever? I know how I got here. I don't know how to get out. Do all survivors experience this trauma? It can't be only me. Why not only me? There's only one me. Other people have no doubt parallel emotions, but each of us is unique. Even our pain is unique. I was told that I had a high threshold of pain. This one is almost beyond my endurance, but I am gritting my teeth and holding on by my fingertips.

THE CAT'S MEOW

March 14, 1993

Hi Finian. Hello, did you come to see if I'm all right? Did he send you to check on me?

I'm playing a tape of joyous Hebrew songs. How you would have loved the music. I can see your smile, your sometimes cherubic smile when you felt particularly happy. How sad I am, how devastated I am, that we are not listening to this music together. I want to scream (I do); I want to cry (I do); I want to die (I don't).

Finian comes up the stairs and gives me the eye.

"I'm okay. Did you come up to see if I was all right?"

I'm not all right, but I will eventually settle down and resume my nothing existence. Being not altogether altruistic, Finian decided he needed a little more food. I obliged. He hung around for a while and I said, "Okay, you can go out with your friends. I'll be fine."

He gave me his penetrating, searching look. He lingered for another ten to fifteen minutes and finally I said, "Go on, it's okay," and he made a mad sprint in the air and went down the stairs back to his cat life.

HOPSCOTCH

March 14, 1993

Did you ever play hopscotch when you were young? I don't know whether children are still playing this game. Probably, but I haven't seen anyone on the sidewalks jumping on one foot, then another and finally both feet placed strategically in position.

"Step on a crack, and you'll break your mother's back."

What a sadistic statement. I must have said those words hundreds of times and looking back I never thought about my mother on her back. It was just the hopping and the care taken to avoid the cracks (lines dividing the square of the sidewalks). It was the skill, the balance required. Whatever it was it was fun and exciting.

I am now back to playing hopscotch, but it's a completely different game. No hopping or jumping in the physical sense, but a tremendous amount of avoiding the cracks emotionally. Step on a crack now and I become disappointed and hurt. I should have avoided the crack. I'm becoming more expert at this mental hopscotch. I'm sure some people have an innate ability to avoid the cracks, but I really wasn't out on the sidewalk of life much. I am learning how to avoid the cracks. It's tricky. You have to be on guard (which is a complete turnaround of my temperament).

Since I haven't played the game literally and figuratively for many years, I'm a little rusty. Now that I'm learning the hazards of this game, I think I can avoid most of the cracks. A mistake now and then will only enhance my awareness. The games have begun; bring on the participants, and may the best man or woman win!

Isn't it funny, isn't it strange that I have to go so far back in my memory to bring me up to date about an age-old game, of which has been played one way or another since the beginning of time?

SEAMINGLESS

March 15, 1993

It is almost five months since you died. You died October 16, 1992. I have to write it down to make it believable and it is still just a date on paper to me. I know you are gone, but I can't accept it. The last few days I'm coming apart at the seams. I've been with people, I've had dinner with people, I've talked to people. You are not here. There is a "red flag" in my line of vision at all times. I'm a fictitious toreador and trying to attract the bull. Do I want to kill the bull or do I want it to kill me? Sometimes I don't seem to know the difference.

I am trying to listen to some joyous folk music. All I can think about is how you would enjoy it. No matter what I do, you are included and then I realize you are not there and I don't know how I can go on. I just keep doing, moving; all so meaningless, so trivial. I am sure if you were alive, we would have shared many of these moments and talked and laughed about them.

I cannot share anything with anybody else. Of course I share, but the depth is shallow. I know it's probably my fault. I want to go swimming with others, hypothetically, of course. I want to feel the waves, the warm water, the exhilaration of water splashing on my face. All I feel is a dry wind. I've turned in all directions, but I cannot seem to capture a cool breeze.

I'm coming apart at the seams. I'm holding myself together, but you have no idea how hard it is. I'm a very inadequate seamstress, so I'm just basting the seams together. Maybe they'll hold. I don't know. Much of the time I don't care.

I hope I can come to some accommodation with your departure from this earth. The above is such a formal sentence, it has absolutely no relation to how I feel. It's just a paper sentence.

Please help me get a handle on life, someone, something, please help!

A BIT OF THEATRICS

March 16, 1993

Everybody's got their "shtick," a Jewish slang word for eccentricity.

My cat likes to drink his water in the bathroom. I can put water next to his food on the kitchen floor where he eats. On rare occasions, I'll see him surreptitiously drink some. Mostly, he follows me into the bathroom and cries piteously. Okay. I bring the water into the bathroom where he drinks enormous amounts, literally hasn't drank for days in his sojourn across the desert of my house. He is now carefully surveying the landscape as he emerges from the bathroom. All clear, he ventures as far as the hall where he proceeds with his grooming. His thirst now quenched, he dashes madly down the stairs and begins his adventures of the day.

We each have our own shtick. I wonder what mine is. What is my typical personal feature? I can think of some general characteristics, but my cat came dashing madly back into the room and now out. Maybe he knows my shtick. If only he could talk. He's lived with me for over eleven years so he knows me the best. There he goes again, madly running into the bedroom, onto the bed. He never does this. I think he's trying to fill me in on my behavior. Well, for once he's right. I do always make the bed. I don't particularly do any household chore daily, but I do make the bed. Okay, Finian (my cat's name), but what is my most theatrical bit?

He is sitting on my unmade bed. It's early yet. Now he dashes out. He's giving me clues, but this scavenger hunt for my shtick still evades me. Life is a shtick. Is that the answer? Not only my life, but all lives are just the total of small roles in the theater of life. How profound that sounds. I'm not one for profundities. I can't, for the life of me, pin point my shtick. I know I talk to strangers sometimes at length. I know there has always been a churning inside of me, a desire to do something or go somewhere. My engine is still running. I think when I was conceived and molded and brought forth unto this world, using the analogy of a machine, the power switch was left in the "on" position. With great effort, I can slow it down, but I can never turn it off.

Maybe that's my shtick. Believe me, this is not one of the greatest things in life to keep running, even when you are asleep or alone. The benefits have helped me along the way. I've never been withdrawn or filled with self pity. I guess my destiny, like it or not, is to live out my life with the power switch on.

Now my cat is howling. I think his power switch is on more often than other cats. I just went out into the living room and petted him on his head. He meowed his approval and I think he said in cat language. "We're two of a kind. We're both restless, we're both clean and we're both on." I think that's what he said. I just gave him some Irish cream, without Bailey's. Tomorrow is St. Patrick's day and with a name like Finian McLonergan, he has the right to celebrate a day early.

MIRIAM AND HER DAUGHTERS

March 16, 1993

It won't be the first time I've seen Miriam, but I have never met the daughters. I'm getting dressed and will soon depart on my new day, meet new people and if I have something to say, I will continue this piece; if not, my pen and hand had a short work out.

We all talked and ate and drank vodka gimlets. We had great Italian food. We don't know each other yet we're exchanging words, but we haven't arrived at a point where we can exchange a deeper mutual friendship. This is a beginning, perhaps not an end but continuum of a friendship has to evolve more slowly to be more lasting. There are exceptions but all of us are starting late in life and we have excess baggage to handle before opening up more to new friends.

I always take my baggage with me but it doesn't stop me from accepting other people and their baggage into my life. I have a big storeroom in which to leave whatever they are carrying, it can always be picked up when they leave. In fact the contents of our baggage has enriched our lives even if we are not aware of the positive aspect of life's burdens. An unlined face hasn't lived and unbending posture hasn't carried any meaningful baggage.

SAINT PATRICK'S DAY

March 17, 1993

I think St. Patrick was the saint who drove the snakes out of Ireland. It is very fitting that today, I am taking my stake in hand and becoming a member of the Out-tough club. I have always been suppliant in the face of tougher opponents. It wasn't worth the fight. It was never a fight for survival, mostly a fight for my own ideas or just something as simple as where to have lunch.

Now that I am alone in this big, big world, I am facing more opponents, more powerful, i.e., Corporations, businesses, etc. Now that I am alone, I am taking my stake in hand and am preparing to drive out the snakes (as St. Patrick drove out the heathens, non-believers). I have my own cause to champion and that cause is "me." It will be the biggest challenge of my life.

I am preparing to do battle; I am prepared to lose some but in the end, I intend to be a winner. I've been out-toughed all my life. Perhaps, not ground to dust under the heels of the tough but certainly bruised, chased away and I have taken refuge in hiding and peeking out when all is clear.

No more, St. Patrick, we may not have the same goals but we, you and your time and me, now, are going to drive out the demons which in my case is my own inner fears of my inability to take charge and use whatever methods are available and not be reduced to impotency. Here I come, world, watch out, this is a force to be reckoned with—high and mighty words from a neophyte in the battle of life. It's never too late to learn and I am a quick study.

WATER TABLE

March 17, 1993

They say water seeks its own level. I'm certainly in the seeking mode; the level which will be my own is unfathomable to me as is my knowledge of how many stars in the sky or how many birds fly. I just realized I made a small poem. Seeking your own level.

In some ways, I've been looking all my life, but since I was in the safe zone of life, the comfort mode, or as some would say "stuck in a rut," I don't even know if the method I am using to find my own level is the right one. Actually, I didn't pick the method; the method picked me. I seem to be following some rambling path that winds and twists, goes up hills and down into valleys. There are no road signs. I have no idea of my destination, but oddly enough I don't really care. I'm following my nose, so to speak, sometimes in a careless manner, sometimes a little more aware of my meanderings. I am seeking my own level. Maybe I have many levels or maybe none at all.

I am not water, but I can feel the flow within me. Sometimes a gentle bubbling spring and at times a fast moving stream graduating to a roaring river. I prefer the waters of the spring. There are not as demanding and I have yet to identify the me who is seeking and the level which may never be realized. If I reread this short essay, I probably would not be able to verbalize the true meaning, but the seeker inside me understands full well what I am talking about.

PSALM OF HELEN

March 19, 1993

Last night when I was asleep, I awoke at brief moments and felt little stirrings, stirrings of life. I was very tired when I went to bed, literally exhausted from a day of a lunch with strangers. All well dressed and polite, a bunch of carefully arranged, meticulously groomed, not a real live one among them. Of course, they were alive, but to me there were inordinately stultifying. I know I haven't been alive either, but I never lived in their world and, of course, they never lived in mine.

I moved away from them as soon as it was socially acceptable and talked at length to a woman who, though we don't agree politically, we agree on a literary and emotional basis. Then I moved on to shopping and met another woman and we talked at length. We had some commonality, but mostly I think we live at different ends of the universe. Home at last, home at last. I was totally exhausted and didn't want to eat though I had a bar of candy. Did not want to read, did not want to watch television. I did have a phone call from a young, energetic woman who is doing her best to live and is going forward. I was so tired. So tired and then to bed. Each time I awoke during the night, I have these small stirrings of life for the first time in a long time. I don't know whether they will grow and I will become a viable person again. By that I mean someone who can care and love someone deeply again. I hope so. I don't know. Maybe these past months have been like a "baptism by fire." I have walked through the valley of the shadow of death and though I fear no evil, I would only hope as it is written in the twenty-third Psalm of David that "goodness and mercy shall follow me all the days of my life."

I would like to add my own words to this Psalm; "let love again enter my heart, let my tears cause the desert within my soul to bloom again and fill me with life and joy."

OVER THE HILL AND THROUGH THE WOODS

March 20, 1993

Warning! Get off the roller coaster! You're going too fast! Slow down real slow. Remember the limerick which is probably only remembered by a few, "Railroad crossing, look out for the cars, can you spell that without any R's?" and of course the answer was to spell "THAT."

I'm getting warning signs, extreme weariness, shortness of breath, lack of interest in doing anything around the house and a constant malaise. I've still been charging ahead, around and back to square one. "Around and round she goes and where she stops, nobody knows." Why are all these childhood rhymes coming to mind now? I guess my intelligent subconscious self is communicating with me on a level it thinks I can relate to; for example, humorous anecdotes and poems. I will slow down, I am talking to myself. I must slow down. I've been test driving myself at an accelerated speed. I can still run, but I have to put parameters around my destinations. Don't go any further than necessary and when you feel your engine beginning to falter, give it a rest. It's probably good for a lot of miles, but you can't abuse the machine that is you. It's amazing that with all the mileage I've accumulated the last few months, the only thing I've really achieved is I can spell "THAT."

Answers are usually simple. It's not necessary to go into depth about the meaning of life or death. At this point, I will speak when spoken to, go somewhere when invited, stay home and learn to live with loneliness and enjoy the luxury of reading again and allow the quiet around me to bring peace instead of panic. I know this won't happen overnight, but today is the beginning of the rest of my life. If I don't want to spin off into space, I better listen to my inner voice: "Take it easy, take it easy." Right!

MY HANDS ARE FULL

March 21, 1993

I'm holding up your end. Isn't it strange that at the end of a life, someone is left holding up both ends. I have to be somewhat ambidextrous, but I've been putting in a lot of practice time for several years, so this juggling act I am now engaged in is not totally new to me. The hardest part is not having someone to tell "Look at me, I'm handling it well" and then knowing you are not handling it all that well; yes, I'm handling it, but what am I handling?

I'm sailing along through the minutes, the hours, the days, the weeks and now the months and there is no one to talk to, really talk to.

I've had more conversations with more people than I've had in years, but I have no one to talk to. You were my only someone and all I can talk to in your place is our cat, Finian. We shared most of our lives together, our trips (small and large), our meals, our purchases, our homes, our differences, our thoughts, our sicknesses and wellness, but the common denominator that is left is Finian.

I can hear you saying as you looked at him, "Didn't I pick out a beauty?" and of course he always added while smiling at me, "I picked you out, too!"

His love for Finian was complete. His love for small creatures was devoid of any dramatics. He just loved small creatures. "Finian, you are a handsome devil. Sweetheart, hello, sweetheart," he said (with the Humphrey Bogart voice).

How I miss you and all there was of you. If I tried to add it up, the sum total would still not be accurate. I would have forgotten another set of figures represent the "you" that I knew. I have been lucky. Not too many people have had anyone like "you." Maybe they could not have appreciated the complicated person you were. You were not easy to fathom. I'm sure I missed some of your angles, but it doesn't matter because in my mind's eye I saw your essence which was unlike anyone else's in the world and will never be seen again. Meanwhile, back at the farm you bought, I'm holding on.

YOU'RE MY TURTLEDOVE

March 22, 1993

You're my little who's it
You're my turtledove
You're my little what's it
You're the One I love.

You used to sing this to Finian (our cat). He usually glanced up in his bored cat face, but every now and then, I thought I detected a glimmer of a very pleased look. You don't know about cats and if they really care. You don't know about people either and if they really care. At least a cat doesn't talk pleasantries so you can't be deceived. With the human race, it's cat of a different color.

I went on my "widow's walk" today. This is a group of new and old widows who meet to talk monthly. Group therapy of a sort. The ones who have been widowed for many years give comfort and support to those who have just entered the realm of widowhood. I feel empathy for all the new ones and the older ones, but I don't fit the mold. I am a widow. I do grieve. I do talk at the meetings but it seems that I am making small talk and it has no relation to their emotions or even mine.

It's like a "day at the races." You go, you watch. Sometimes you win, sometimes you lose. In this case, the winning would be to leave a meeting with a feeling of well being, if even temporary. The losing would be that you leave the meeting without having gained any benefits, other than being out for the day.

I am a loser. I gain nothing. The conversation is diluted between the participants; one sobs, one empathizes, one relates how she feels, one relates how she felt years before. It's a well meaning group. I'm sure there are some winners. Maybe since I don't like to lose, I feel this group has little to offer me.

I need to be out in the world. I need the conversation of all peoples. I need to be needed. I don't know how much I have to give or how much I want to give, but in the meantime I'm moving about in the horse latitudes. I don't look forward to another day, but I don't hide from it either. Most days I don't plan, some I do. It's like getting dressed. What am I going to wear? I open the closet and sooner or later put together my wardrobe for the day. That is how I go forward. I open the closet of my mind and arrange my thoughts and actions for the next few hours. Each day is the same. Maybe I've been doing something like this all my life, but being busy with so many urgencies, I did not realize subconsciously I was keeping my house in order in a similar fashion. Now I have many quiet hours, alone hours and I am coming to terms with what is. I can still smile and remember you singing though:

> Who's your little who's it
> Who's your turtledove
> Who's your little what's it
> Who's the one I love!

SEDUCTION OF SILENCE

March 24, 1993

And so it continues, to sleep if you can, to wake if you must. The pattern of life is routine. There are variations on the theme, but the hours go by for all of us. Last night as I was talking on the phone, I began speaking of the seduction of silence. I have no idea where this term came from, original or not, but then I began to think on it. Since I've only just begun the silence of living alone, I realized that the seduction does take place. Slowly at first, never overwhelming, but in its own way insidious. Firstly, when it overtakes you, you want to shake it off like a dog that has just come in from the rain.

But it's not about to go away. It has moved into your life, and your home. Silence has now become a member of your family. First thing is to run away from it and eventually you begin to make your peace with it. It hasn't happened yet, but at times I almost feel happy in its presence. It allows me time to think, to reminisce, to feel emotions that perhaps I've felt before, but not in their entirety. The loneliness of silence, the becoming aware is akin to the beginning of a love affair. It contains the unknown, the mystery, the tantalizing prospect of something more interesting that will be revealed in time. It is also maddening in its reclusive silence.

It is necessary to not fight the inevitably of the outcome. I have a tendency to grit my teeth and clench my fists and try and ignore this new presence that has entered my life. Whether it becomes my friend or enemy, I know depends entirely on me. But at this point, I am not ready to make a commitment.

GO FOR IT

March 27, 1993

I might be over the hill but I'm not through the woods. When I was younger, there were no hills on my horizon, only stretches of long, long views without end. When I saw a hill I went around it, admiring its height, its changing colors in the light of morning or dusk.

I know how to traverse the hills, but the woods are still a dark, foreboding place to me literally and figuratively. I think I have quite a few hills in my future. I think I will be able to appreciate the views from my vantage point in life. I'm not ready for the woods. Obviously, I won't have any choice.

When the time comes and the only exit from this life and into the next one is a stand of trees all huddled together making it impossible to see what is beyond them if anything at all, I want to remember the sunrise, I want to remember.

One of the new words classified as a form of discrimination is "ageism." I have begun to feel this "ageism" these last years. Not in its total discriminatory meaning, just little tidbits: not being taken seriously, when I'm serious, being slightly ignored, but not completely. So far I've not let it get to me, but the "me" that I'm becoming has decided to not let "them" intimidate the "me" that has gotten older.

Senility is not reserved for the older person, many younger people have all the symptoms of senility. For example, forgetfulness, indifference, lack of interest, self-involvement, diminished initiative, I could go on and on. "Ageism" is a figment of one generation's imagination of what older people have degenerated into. Some simple, unsophisticated stage where they have become a burden on society. The only asset they possess (if they do) is their estate which can be passed on to enhance the lives of these viable, intelligent, important people who think they are contributing to someone or something and making this a better world. While their older counterparts are just putting in shortened hours, doing frivolous or meaningless things awaiting the approach of the grim reaper.

Wake up, wake up! All ye who can hear. We're all awaiting the approach of the grim reaper. We who are intelligent, stay intelligent. We, who are viable, stay viable. To add a little extra, we have had many more years of experience and have honed our skills. Be it as simple as a household chore, or as complicated as a scientific equation.

I say eliminate all "-isms." They are too numerous to enumerate. I say experience the joy of all ages, all cultures, to share with those who have the ability to partake of the luxury of life. Life is much too short for all of us. I am trying to make the rest of my life as full as possible. What it will be full of depends upon the ingredients that come within my grasp.

"Oh ye of little faith..." Have faith in your future. Live in the present but keep an eye out so you don't miss any opportunities for happiness, for knowledge, for adventure. Don't dash madly into the unknown, but don't resort to retiring into the comfort of the "old shoe" syndrome.

In my case, my spirit is willing, but sometimes my physical self is a little shopworn and tired. The trick of the trade is balance. Sometimes on the tightrope of life I teeter, but I don't fall and sometimes I just come down and give myself a breather until I feel ready for another try. This I must do, I must always try. No one will ever be able to say "she didn't try." "She always went for it." Not a bad eulogy.

WHAT SHALL I DO NOW THAT YOU'RE FAR AWAY, WHAT SHALL I DO?

March 28, 1993

Now comes the mornings of my discontent. I think my days have been filled with these little devils draining my energy. I have ignored their pernicious habits and have blithely wended my ways past the hours. This morning came as no surprise to me, yet I cannot make any decisions at all. Do I want to go out? Do I want to stay home? Do I want to be with people and if so, how many? Do I feel well, do I not feel well enough to do something, anything? What is this all about? Am I evolving into a mass of indecisiveness and will I ever be able to make a decision?

I can't sit, stand or move around the house in this mental maze. I sit myself down, I write it all down and see where I am heading. I have things to do next week. Ordinary, but important things which I will do. What about the days that need to be used up? The hours that need to be filled? I can't lay down on the job and sleep away the time. I couldn't do this even if I chose to. Daytime sleeping has never been my thing or escape and I'm not about to start now. Do I want to wander around today, looking at art, having small conversations? Do I want company and have the presence of other living, breathing entities inhabiting my space for a while? Either of these decisions would be acceptable, but as Freud said, "What do women want?" but he wasn't referring to my kind of woman.

I'm a woman on the edge (a new widow). We have a special place in the world, a very special place. We are the survivor of a marriage, where our mate is dead and we are left to face the music. I don't hear music, I don't even hear. It seems to me that all is left of me, at least for the time being, is emotion. Many lows, some highs, and a tremendous emptiness. My cup runneth over and now there is nothing left but an empty cup.

THE GREGARIOUS RECLUSE

March 30, 1993

I seem to be divided into two people, totally unrelated to each other. I have always been this way but have never thought about this particular type of dichotomy. When I'm out, when I'm in the company of people, I am vocal, cheery, devil-may-care, you name it. If I'm not the life of the party, I'm a very active participant.

When I'm alone, I can review these actions and wonder what I was all about. Was as I happy as I seemed? Was I as amusing as I thought I was, and what in the devil was I talking about so madly and so gladly? Here I am now, alone and I haven't a clue where I was coming from. It seems that my gregarious self has always been running away from my reclusive self, and vice-versa.

I suppose the answer could be oversimplified and described as "it's just your nature, personality or genetic makeup." I know it's not easy to define, I even know it's not that important to analyze this behavior. I know though, at times, this is disturbing; a sort of schizoid person who doesn't seem to fit in any world, not in this world. Again I would hope to find a few people who, though they may be totally unlike this, will enjoy the gregarious and empathize with the recluse. Of all the millions of people on this planet, there must be a few that understand the "me" I don't understand. I wish I could meet some of them, even one of them.

Before I die I need to know who I am. Of course, I suppose I'll just keep on being this gregarious recluse and not dwell on it too much. My actions at times are maddening even to myself. I don't want to drive the world away nor do I want to spin off into deep space or fall into deep despair. "Have a good day."

STAR BRIGHT, STAR LIGHT

March 31, 1993

I am the light-heavyweight of the world in my class. I realized yesterday that beyond the happy-go-lucky aura I exude most times when I am out and about there lurks a very sober and somber persona, bewildered by the politics of the world, saddened by my inability to do anything that will be beneficial to mankind. This heavyweight is new to me. It's always been around, but it never reared its heavy head until lately.

It's better to meander through your life, as if you were taking a walk in a park or a garden. Now that this dark, brooding thinking self has emerged, what do I do about it? I need more facts and information so when it takes center stage, there will be an informed self; not a partially developed thought.

I have to be more definitive. I have to stand up for my ideas and ideals regardless of the consequences. I have to have more courage than I have ever had in my life. I have to go forward and the devil take the hindmost. This is a challenge I don't relish, but if I want to be this new light-heavyweight champion in my class, I have to accept the risks. What could be so difficult? I will make some enemies and perhaps some friends. I will have gained more respect if not from others, from myself. I'm not a fighter, but a battle doesn't have to be fought with fists and guns, a real battle is fought with the mind. Now is my chance to gain a title I never dreamed I would achieve or have ever imagined existed.

Again, I say to myself, "Ye, of little faith..." (in yourself), go forth and slay the dragons that surround your moat. This all sounds very dramatic, but life is the real drama. We watch actors from our seats in theaters and in our homes, and never realize we are the real actors going from one scene to another. Sometimes the scene is a repetition of one we've been in before but if we are truly aware, there are always nuances that give each scene a different meaning.

All our lives we play the same character, but as on the stage we grow older, more mature. Sometimes we don't grow wiser, but we do change subtly or drastically depending upon the events in our lives that shape us. We all consist of dough-like substance. Our face and bodies change over the years and if we are lucky, our perception and awareness become more acute and astute. We begin to like ourselves more at times and realize that the aging process has its own advantages.

The deep, deep sorrow is that all those who have died have taken their enlightened minds with them into the darkness and those of us who are left have to light our own fires and replenish the warmth that we once felt from their afterglow.

"Tiger, tiger, burning bright
In the forest of the night,
What immortal hand or eye
Could frame thy fearful symmetry?"

APRIL FOOL

April 1, 1993

I'm not such a big shot. Boy, am I not. I'll have to amend my journal dated March 22, 1993, re: my widow's walk and the negative impact it had on me. I realized today that I do not want to accept the fact that my husband is gone forever, dead forever.

By attending these meetings I am in a sense being disloyal by admitting to myself that I am one of them. I'm okay. I'm doing everything fine. I'm driving, going shopping, meeting people, having lunches, dinners. I'm making plans of a sort but I'm not really a widow, am I? I haven't cried, or very little. I'm big and strong, aren't I? "Look ma, I'm dancing (as the old expression goes)."

Yes, I'm dancing. Actually I'm running away from myself and my emotions. I'm doing fine. Every night when I go to bed, I touch your side of the bed and tell you good night and then my mind is screaming, "You're not gone, you're not gone! It's impossible, how could you be gone?"

I eventually settle down and go to sleep, dozing off and thinking, "How could this have happened?" Sure I know people die, but not you. Not my husband. Not the person I shared a lifetime with. Sometimes I want desperately to be dead with you, but I'm dead enough as it is. This cheerful, happy, talkative person the world sees is not dead. It is only the "me" I live with that moves about the house that is barely alive. I'm a busy ghost, or what would you call us? I have been told by friends that there will come a time that I will be at peace with myself. It is called being focused. At the moment, I most certainly am out of focus. I will keep putting on the brave front.

Very few will know unless they read this that at the moment I am like a stage set. I am surrounding myself with fake props. The "me" on stage in front of the audience (the world outside my home), is not aware that when the curtain comes down, I am totally devoid of the persona I have displayed on the stage of life. This is not totally a new role for me. We all act out roles all through our lives. At the moment, I have assumed the roles of a mother, a sister, a friend and other assorted roles.

But I refuse to play the role of a widow. I refuse to learn the lines. I refuse to accept the part. Today, at this time, I absolutely say "NO" to widowhood.

NOTHING TO DO

April 2, 1993

I have nothing to do
But sit in the shade and think
Of how hot, the day has got
And how the pigs do stink

I don't have any money
I don't have a car
I don't have a handsome boyfriend
I don't look like a movie star

I have nothing to do
But sit in the shade and think
Of how hot, the day has got
And how the pigs do stink

I just remembered these verses I wrote when I was about thirteen or fourteen years old living in Texas next door to people who kept pigs, chickens and a cow. I don't know why I remembered this silly poem now, except I can relate to the first line, "I have nothing to do."

At least during those years, I was very young and probably only felt that way for a few hours. I don't remember. I do remember I was a lonely child and read continuously. I spent my summer vacations at the public library which was like a wonderful castle to me full of delights for the mind. I went from fairy tales on up to so many books; I can't remember any titles. Books were my best friends through my growing-up years.

They have befriended me since, but not at the intense level they did so long ago. I wish it would be as easy to become engrossed in reading now, but my attention span is fragmented. After a few pages, my mind wanders off. I try to bring it back to attention, but it refuses to stay in one place, on one line or one page. I just let it go wandering. It won't go far, but I don't know when it will settle down and concentrate again. I suppose I'll just have to sit in the shade and think of how hot the day has got, and maybe have a drink.

Now I have enough money
I even have a car
My handsome boyfriend died
He looked like a movie star!

HE'S BACK

April 3, 1993

He's back, he's back. Finian hurried up the back steps up into the house. He had heard sounds coming from upstairs and I was talking to him from the back door so he knew it wasn't me. He's back, oh joy. As he ran into the house, I picked him up as I knew he was going to be devastated when he found out you were not back. It was a stranger in the house. I had hired someone to clean and I knew when he saw her, he would madly run away.

Of course, as I carried him up the stairs, your scent was nowhere and he began to get nervous. When he saw the stranger, he panicked and took off like you used to say, "...like a ruptured duck." He has been doing this for months.

A sound.

You're back, where are you? Animals know many things and sense many things, but death is not in their consciousness. We are the only living being that knows we are going to die and we are aware of death. Most of the time, in order to keep our sanity, we don't think about death, ours or our loved ones. Poor Finian. He looked so animated upon hearing the sounds in the house and how can I explain death to our cat? I talk to him about you. I want you back as much as he does. Oh, how I want you back. Is Finian doomed to come looking for you every time a new sound comes from our house? Will he accept the inevitability of your death? I doubt it. I know we die, and I have not accepted it yet and probably never will. There will always be a hole in my heart that aches for you. Time might heal, but never totally and for the years I have left, I want to feel your presence even if I will never see you again.

Poor Finian. Poor me. We survivors carry a sad burden of memories.

PAIN PILLS

April 4, 1993

I know that prescriptions, i.e., pills, are either generic or by brand names. Supposedly, there should not be much difference but there is usually; it is the filler that is added to generic, making it inferior, thereby producing a less effective drug. I am sure there are other subtle changes. The reason I am talking about pills, generic or otherwise, is that I realize my life has become generic.

The places I go, the meals I eat, the people I meet are all generic. I am looking for a panacea for my pain, but I can't find the real thing. Maybe there is no name brand to help me relieve my pain and I have no choice but to take the drugs available to me which are all generic. Some work better than others; some of the ingredients produce at least a temporary relief from my pain. The pain of losing one's husband. The pain of not always knowing what to do or how to do it without talking it over with your life long companion. At least I can rely on my generic resources without which I would have no respite from my inner anguish.

As I look over tonight at my furry friend, Finian (our cat), I guess he is not generic. He's the real thing. He is probably the realest thing in my life. He's lying peacefully next to me after a good meal and small wash up of his face and he's totally cat. No imitation of himself; absolutely the real thing. I am grateful for my generic life until I can start living truly in whatever "real life" is ahead of me. I'll accept these substitutes and for all I know they will be as effective to ease my pain and help me on the road to recovery.

PSYCHOBABBLE

April 6, 1993

"Reading and writing and 'rithmetic
Learned to the tune of a hick'ry stick."

I've been reading an article about psychobabble. We've been inundated with these words for years. Vocabulary as follows: (Evil, bad)—judgment is very impaired; (Rage)—overreaction; (Solution to family problems)—find a way to emotionally empower that tie between parents; (Mistakes)—error in judgment.

Yikes! Gadzooks! How far have we traveled down the road from common sense to verbal nonsense? When I went school, we were never hit with a hick'ry stick or was there one in evidence? We were taught to read and write and do math. Along the way we were exposed to rational thinking by our teachers and our peers. We learned about being bad, about rage, anger and mistakes. None of us were immune from all of the above. We did learn and grow and mature but for the most part we lived a happy and productive life.

We all had parents, sometimes one who had to take the place of two. Even when there were two we usually only took one seriously (the one who was the most compatible with the way we felt then). If my parents could ever find a way to "emotionally empower their tie," they would not know what these words meant. They were much too busy working, taking care of all the daily needs required of parents, care and feeding of family which filled all the hours of the day. Indeed "empower their tie." They were married and lived together. There weren't tied.

"Empower." How high-sounding this word, but what is the literal definition? Random House Dictionary: "to give power or authority; to enable or permit." My mother, so to speak, would stop whatever she was doing and say to my father, "You have my permission to mow the lawn."

My father would then say to my mother, "I would enjoy fried chicken tonight."

See, it's real easy! Of course my father might not have mowed the lawn and my mother might not have made fried chicken, but obviously they were "empowering" each other to make choices which they could or could not do. Obviously, they were "emotionally empowering their tie." I wonder if there will come a day when we return to the early speech patterns of my day. Past the double-speak, past the psychobabble. I know they will have to define it. Let me think "realistic interaction," or "fundamental basics." I don't care what it is called. I like "down to brass tacks," but I know that is much too simplistic for this age of unreason. So in final analysis, I'm back to square one:

> "Reading and writing and 'rithmetic
> Learned to the tune of a hick'ry stick."

DAMNED SPOT

April 9, 1993

Out, damned spot! Out, I say!

I am not Lady Macbeth, nor did I participate in the dying, but now I'm trying to remove the stains that remind me of you. Not you yourself, but the spots that remain here and there throughout the house. All the storing of unneeded objects, all saving of things we might use again, all the things we just might need. The removal of these spots lessens the harsh reality of your death. I must bring new things into my life and settle in with the rest. I can do this, but when I discard some of the excess around me, I feel good. The stain is not gone, but it is dimming. When we die, we leave a huge spot and those of us who are left have to diminish the pain we live with by change; a little at first and then we notice the spot grows smaller. I know it will never go away nor do I want it to. I would like to quote from Macbeth, Act IV:

"Tomorrow, and to-morrow, and to-morrow
Creeps in this petty pace from day to day
To the last syllable of recorded time;
And all our yesterdays have lighted fools
The way to dusty death. Out, Out brief candle!
Life's but a walking shadow, a poor player
That struts and frets his hour upon the stage
And then is heard no more; it is a tale
Told by an idiot, full of sound and fury,
Signifying nothing."

Ah, if I could write like that! But how lucky that I am that I'm still here to read it!

THE CAT'S AWAY

Easter Sunday—April 11,1993

"When the cat's away, the mice will play." Today I'm all dressed up. My usual attire is casual, very casual. I'm going to have brunch with a group of women at an elegant place. I'm looking forward to it. But my cat's away (you were the smartest, most handsome Tom that ever crossed my path) and how lucky I was that you decided I was the one you wanted to spend your life with! The rest of us are scurrying around like mice, working, keeping busy, just doing our time on earth in the best way we know how.

Fortunately, things break and have to be fixed. Yards fill with weeds and have to be tended, clothes need washing and repairing, food needs to be bought and cooked, and on and on it goes (our scurrying). Even our bodies need a little tender, loving care by doctors who are well paid, but nevertheless share in our maintaining our heath. Oh how busy we are, how busy.

Well, Tom, you did your busy time, you certainly did your share of all the scurrying. We "mice," are still scrambling about. I seem to view you in retrospect as this large creature who could handle anyone and anything. You always seemed bigger than life. You had such assurance, such a take-charge air. I miss you as I go scurrying about, but I must play, I really must. As I embark on each new venture, the phrase always goes through my mind, "Here goes nothing; it really doesn't matter; it should be interesting to see what happens." Words to live by. Actually this has been my creed all my life, but I have to bring them to the forefront of my mind so I will not regress into self-pity (a very poor companion).

SOUNDS IN THE NIGHT

April 14, 1993

I heard you the night before last. I heard something in the house. It was a sound unlike anything I can describe. A moving sound, not too loud, but enough to wake me out of a shallow sleep. I checked out my cat. He was sound asleep on the couch. I went back to bed after checking around the house. Again, I heard the sound. I got up and looked around again. Then I noticed I had forgot to turn off the VCR; the lights were shining brightly. I turned it off and back to bed. No more sounds. I wondered, it is possible you were telling me to turn off the set. Is it possible for you to communicate with me by reminding, "you left the light on"?

We both at different times gave each other orders (not aggressively), just the kind of give and take in a marriage. Did you buy that? Did you forget to get something or other? And of course, the perennial question asked over and over the generations. Did you turn off all the lights? I had left the lights on. There is no one to question me anymore and wherever you are, in whatever form you are in, you are still telling me to turn off the lights! I would only wish our communication would go beyond this. I think it does. It seems when I'm not too sure where I am going or what to do, you are there guiding me subconsciously. You installed in me over the years the self-esteem needed to accomplish whatever is necessary. We all need what is now called "stroking" and that you did and I thank you. I am still listening to you as you might not have been aware of when you were a living presence in my life. But I am still listening. As I just told someone yesterday, I learned from the "Master." Whenever I falter on what to do, immediately comes to my mind, "what would he have done?." Then I try to emulate your strength and go forward in my actions.

Running in place is no solution, only an exercise in futility. If you are going to run or walk or even crawl, move forward. Mistakes are forgiven, but inaction is not only pointless, but cowardly. Thank heaven for strong men and strong women. They do live after they are gone. They live with those they left behind and help them cope all the days of their lives. If I ever leave the lights on or need to be reminded of something I've neglected, please come back and alert me. As long as I know someone will come back and nudge me to awareness, I welcome any form or sound you choose. Just please come back, please come back.

FINE AND DANDY

April 14, 1993

There is a comedian whose response to every question is "Fine and dandy." I can see his silly smile, his seemingly benevolent face and his voice saying in an oily tone, "Fine and dandy."

When people ask me how I feel or how I liked something, at the back of my mind is this voice saying, "Fine and dandy." I do use the word "fine" a lot, but "dandy," never. It is a perfectly good word, though obsolete in these days of words like "cool," "chill out," to replace the older ones like "smooth," "bugged out," or "bummer." "Fine" seems to still be in usage by many, so I feel "fine." Why do we have to define how we feel or where we go? Why can't we ignore our feelings and just go into the specifics like, "I feel better today than yesterday," and "I like the restaurant and maybe the next one I will like even better." Why are answers so often confined to the isolation of one word, "Fine," or in the case of the comedian, "Fine and Dandy"?

We have dictionaries full of thousands of words, Roget's Thesaurus giving us a multitude of words to describe one. Back to the real world of monosyllabic answers. We no longer converse, we evade intimacy. Are we afraid of becoming emotionally involved with ourselves? I am so grateful that my life is not reduced to "fine and dandy." As much as I don't want to feel pain, it is much better to be vulnerable and feel than be invulnerable and retreat into the inner self. By being me, I can be "fine and dandy" when I am, and anything else when I'm not.

COBBLESTONES

April 15, 1993

As I was talking yesterday, I realized my words, my vocabulary, certain words with specific meanings were like cobblestones on a street. Each time I used these words, I could feel my mind start stepping from stone to stone on a journey whose destination remains a mystery. The final destination is on the map for all of us, but our travels until then is a search for understanding, awareness and beauty. I love words, I love traveling, I love searching. The more words I can use to express my thoughts, the further down the cobblestones I will travel.

I always thought of travel as a physical entity; the itinerary into a foreign place, the transport of my physical being and the newness of something I've never seen. This is travel, of course, but now I realize there are other trips to take. The adventures of the mind are never-ending. The only luggage you carry is internalized within your mind. The adventures are without number and at any time you can stop and rest.

All these years I've been walking down these cobblestone streets totally unaware of the distance I have traveled. My walks up until now have been erratic. It is not necessary to have a map and be regimented, but the knowledge of these streets is important. I should choose my path more carefully, be more selective of the sites I wish to see and give myself the rest I need to be able to resume my travels. My cobblestones of words: What a delight to identify the streets I've been walking down my whole life.

I AM A CONTENDER

April 15, 1993

You are awfully quiet. You will be gone five months tomorrow. I have been surrounded by the sound and fury I have created to give me solace now that I am alone. You are truly gone. I don't know what you would call this stage. First "anger," then "denial," and now what? Is it acceptance? I think not. Is it a reality check? I think not.

What stage am I entering? The stage of quiet contemplation is part of it. The stage of gathering my inner resources is part of it. Obviously, this is no stage at all. It is simply the beginning of the end of my life. This is not as sad as is sounds.

Since life must end, I am at the beginning which gives me time to develop skills I've never developed; enjoy activities I had no time for, grow into truly my own person for better or worse. But all in all this is a challenge I look forward to. As you would have said, "If you can't be a champion, be a contender." And so it will be.

GOOD-BYE

April 16, 1993

I told you good-bye last night. I did not say "goodnight" as I've been saying these past five months. I said "good-bye."

I'll still be talking to you, asking questions, getting your advice, but I know it is time to say "Good-bye." There are several options open to me. I can still hope to see you again if there is another again for us. I can still feel your strength and intelligence when it comes time for me to make a decision. I can still appreciate your generosity when I feel frivolous about spending money. I can try to visualize how you would react to situations which I will be facing in the future.

I will try to make you proud of me. How comforting it is to be able to rely on someone who is gone. You were a good teacher and you taught me how to be self-sufficient. True, I had the inner resources to start with, but I needed someone to give me the self-esteem and courage necessary for the good life.

The good life, not to be interpreted as anything other than truthful, fair and responsible. I want to thank you for being my husband. I want to thank you for all the plaudits you bestowed on me. I want to thank you for so many things!

The rest of my life will be richer and fuller because of you. I am now a peregrinator into the unknown, but I have no fear. You are with me consciously and subconsciously; helping me, comforting me, supporting me.

How odd that now I've told you "good-bye," you've assumed another persona, not godlike, but something akin to an unseen gentle presence that pervades our home.

As I told Finian, our cat, last night—"You are not one of the sweet, passive cats in the world, but when you curl up in my lap at night, I know there is a pussy cat inside the pussy cat!"

No one knew you as I did and inside your strong, intense exterior was the kindest, gentlest man in the world. Sleep well, my gentle love, sleep well.

NOT FORGOTTEN

April 16, 1993

Something keeps nudging me. Something keeps reminding me of you. "*Gone, but not forgotten.*" These words keep intruding in my mind all day. Of course you are gone but not forgotten. Is it necessary to put these words on paper so that they have a place to lay their head?

I keep hearing your voice saying, "I'm dying, I'm dying." As you lay in the hospital. Tears streaming down my face, I can still hear myself saying, "No matter where you are going, I am going to be with you," and so I am. I would wish away your voice, the chant of dying. It still tears at my heart, the helplessness of the still living to witness the dying; and in the dying the total loss of any words of comfort for either you or me.

"*Gone but not forgotten.*" A cliché, an expression meaning many things to many people at many times. Does life boil down to a cliché or is it just an oversimplification of deep emotions? I know the other clichés, too. "*Time heals everything.*" I doubt this one. It is just another pat phrase to try and comfort you. I guess if a few clichés would help, I will gladly be receptive to anything that dulls the pain.

It is mostly your voice that keeps intruding in my waking hours. It is the piteous sound, the questioning I hear in your voice. You want me to say, "No, you're not dying," but I can't speak of that. I cannot lie to you. Do you think someday your voice with the plaintive words, "I'm dying, I'm dying," will be only a distant memory? I do not know. I would hope so.

It is hard to embrace the life I still have with the thoughts of your cries in my ears. I need more time to mourn, I need more time to cry and then perhaps I can go forward more easily. The joy of living is very fragile when you are suddenly deprived of your partner in life. I know I must go, do and participate in all the living available, but I don't want to hear your voice in my head. You are gone, but not forgotten.

As long as I live you become more alive to me everyday. I quote things you've said, words you used, philosophy you espoused at times, your attitudes toward people and the human condition. You left me a legacy that is remarkable in its plenitude. I am full of you, up to the brim. I can quote you from now until eternity. "Forgotten."

You live in me. You are as much a part of me as my eyes, my ears and all who know me now and in the future will know you not by your name. I have it now, but I always give you the credit when I discuss something meaningful. You were articulate (I am a poor imitation). As another cliché goes, "Imitation is the sincerest form of flattery." Thanks for holding on as long as you could, but let me go now.

MR. UNINVOLVEMENT

April 17, 1993

I was talking to my cat this morning. He turned his back to me which he does most of the time and seemed to forget I existed. At times I find this maddening and insulting, but then I tell myself "he's only a cat!" He doesn't know what I am saying. Actually, I think he does, but doesn't want to acknowledge me.

Even people who don't turn their backs when you are speaking are mostly pretending to listen. There are listeners, but have you ever noticed that when someone is really listening (the key to a listener is if they ask questions relating to the subject you are expounding on at the time), you begin to feel self-conscious and a little embarrassed and wonder if you are talking too much and saying too little?

I am a talker. I am also a listener. My cat has a bit of both, but when it comes to listening I always seem to get the back of his head. Maybe it is a cat's way of telling you to keep on talking and I will call out what I want to hear and let the rest pass. If he is looking at me, that would be an acknowledgment of his ability to listen and understand and as follows, have to ask a question to show his interest. Since we don't talk the same language, he is saving face by refusing to face the issues—me. I admire this trait even though it can be exasperating to feel you are being ignored.

We do not relate deeply on many levels. None verbal, but as long as there is communication, it is good. I sense that he is attuned to my grievances or just my conversation of the moment. I call him at times 'Mr. Uninvolvement,' but it's not really true. He is probably the most involved cat in the world with his owner. I use the word "owner" judiciously. I don't own him per se. We just live together. My "Main" man now and his "Mistress."

DANCING IN THE DARK

April 18, 1993

When I was very small, people would ask me, "What do you want to be when you grow up?"

I unfailingly gave the same answer for many years. "I want to be a dancing girl."

In retrospect, I have been a "dancing girl," but not in the literal sense of the word. I've been bubbling, churning, dashing here and there talking, listening, absorbing and I never realized I had achieved my early ambition. Just as the quote, "A rose by any other name..." so it is for me, a dancing girl on the stage of "life" is where I have performed my "dancing" and I continue to pursue my craft. I think I have it down to a fine art now. Years of practice might not make perfect, but they do allow you to give an acceptable performance.

I only today realized that I was the "dancer," the child that was me dreamed of being. I have many partners to dance with of all ages, sexes, colors and styles. I do love to dance. Sometimes I weary, but a brief respite I'm ready to take to the dance floor again. Dance gypsy, cry gypsy, play while you may!

FISH GOTTA SWIM

April 19, 1993

"Fish gotta swim, birds gotta fly, I gotta love one man till I die."

How true, how true! Words from songs, words from poems, words from books. Someone wrote all these words with someone or something in mind. All these years I've been taking these words at face value. Pleasant, sad, beautiful, or whatever the words conveyed to me at the time. It seems I have just awakened and am hearing and seeing everything in a new light. It's a good light. It shows me a new path that I am following; full of adventure, a deeper understanding and most of all I am filling a need to fulfill my curiosity about almost everything.

I have been living in a cocoon. A loving warm cocoon, but as should happen I am leaving this safe haven and venturing forth into the wide open spaces. How odd that I have the ability at this time in my life to "take wing."

No doubt, I have been waiting at the gate and when it opened after your death, I took the opportunity to venture forth with a vengeance. All my pent-up energy, or whatever it is called, was released. I have had many adventures, met many new people.

I have been giddy at times at the volume of sound I have embraced. I will have to endeavor to put my house in order and be a little more circumspect, but not too much. I have to give myself a wide berth to make mistakes to waste time and even some money, but nothing that will be detrimental to me or others.

As my cat, Finian, sits in the sun by the door gazing intently at the outside and then wanders gracefully through the room, I take my directions from him. Observe, move out and do it graciously and gracefully. Oh Finian McLonergan, you always knew now to live! Animals rarely have the hang-ups we humans have. Maybe I am becoming just "a natural woman," but he was always "a natural cat."

OFF AND RUNNING

April 21, 1993

In about an hour, I'll be off and running. Ever since you died I have been going, going, going, gone. I feel not like I'm at an auction, but that I am one of objects being auctioned off. I go to the highest bidder each day. My calendar fills up each week. Mostly lunch, some dinner, some stay at home and wait for something to get fixed and a few days interspersed with doing nothing or household chores or reading or watching television.

I imagine in time my motor will need a tune-up and I'll take it to the shop. Anyway, for the time being, I'm not having any engine trouble, the tank is full and the driver is willing! Was there always this fire within? Yes there was, but it was necessary to dampen the flames and only let the embers glow. There was no time for racing through the days. There was time for contemplation, there was time for the necessities, but no time for madness like the dashing about, the old newness I had almost forgotten.

Now that my memory is refreshed, I should channel and become more structured. Ha! Me structured? Not a chance! I was born to dance and I am trying out all the new steps I have learned. Maybe I'll become a more accomplished dancer, but it will take age to slow me down and even then, I'll be tapping my toes and moving my hands.

"Old dancers never die, they just move into the audience."

DESULTORY DESOLATION

April 21, 1993

As I awakened this morning, I realized in what a desultory manner I've been moving about. No plan, no purpose; just randomly moving through the day, sometimes with high energy, sometimes not. I suppose I am not unique, but each of us is unique to himself.

To top it all off, they are back—my nightmares, my friends of my youth. They had left me for the past months and I attributed my good fortune of ridding them to the fact that my days had become nightmares, since your death. At least I would have easy sleep. I guess this means I'm getting well, if you want to use this word. My nights are returning to the maze of weird, unpleasant sequences and my grief is being submerged somewhere in my subconscious to surface now and again.

So I go about in desultory desolation, almost smiling, always seemingly happy. I'm fine, just fine. After all, like a dog chases its tail I can chase my moods even if I don't catch them. I hope I can find a direction and not finish my life in this haphazard fashion. Being who I am and what I am, I'll probably never be totally directed. I need a director, but someone I respect implicitly. No play, movie, opera, symphony or ballet is done without a director. He or she is the intrinsic part of a production. My director has retired. I am not on the lookout for one, but if per chance one should appear upon the scene, I would perhaps be willing to take part. I am now under no contract and am freelancing through life.

It will be hard to give up this pseudo freedom. Not too unlike a caged animal who is released into the wild, I feel exhilaration, apprehension, unevenness of the spirit, and a longing to be back in the confines of the safe place I had lived in for many years.

How to adapt to the wild? I have no idea. I guess not to be too curious about what is around the bend, be more circumspect than you would naturally be, but mostly don't let the desire to return to a safe place stymie you in your pursuit of a dream you haven't even dreamed yet!

ALL MY CHILDREN

April 22, 1993

It is a beautiful sunny morning and I am looking out at the city and seeing a myriad of houses, buildings, greenery, streets running up and down with attached cars. I am seeing and feeling the intense joy of living. I am feeling like a mother rejoicing at the accomplishments of her children.

I am wanting to embrace all the people who need love. I am full of desire to become a part of this beautiful scene and share it with those whose view is limited. I wonder if my emotions would have been different if I had had children of my own. No doubt I would have been unable to see the larger picture because my own private world would have been much smaller and more intense. For whatever reason I do not have my own family, I am pleased to be a part of this tremendous, unwieldy panorama.

I can give love and comfort to many. I can share beauty with all who can appreciate it. I can be useful with no strings attached. It is still a big responsibility; I do not take my role lightly. It has to be played with sincerity and compassion. It also needs big doses of humor and you have to know when to leave the stage.

The old adage "Leave them laughing" is a good line, but you also need to leave them wanting more. You don't want the world to tire of you. You don't want to be repetitious. You have to keep creating interesting nuances to your performance. Since the world is my audience and the audience is my "children," I hope to give them some lasting memories of my time on stage. Meanwhile, I love my role. It's the role of a lifetime.

What a remarkable awakening to think that the "mother" within has found a need for her talent, ability or whatever it is that mothers need to fulfill their destiny. We are all mothers and fathers with or without children, married or unmarried. Not all have the time or inclination to discover this intrinsic part of our natures, but I did. How fortunate to find yourself in the complexity of our makeup.

Ah, sweet mystery of life, at last I found you!

OVER THE WIDE BLUE YONDER

April 23, 1993

I seem to be going through metamorphoses on different age levels. I seem to be universal in that I have no age prejudices and adapt to each person at their stage in life. I know I have passed through most of them and I am now regressing selectively. When I'm with someone in their twenties or early thirties I become the giddy, not too sophisticated, earnest someone they are. As I advance in age (ergo companion), I become more sophisticated, more intelligent, a bit cynical, but still filled with the wonder of life.

When I advance past my years and am in the company of those who are not as physically or mentally viable as they used to be, I am the surrogate daughter, sister or friend who can help them in small ways they are no longer able to do or perhaps never could.

How amazing that death forced me out of my cocoon and has turned into a butterfly-like creature. I am flitting about and landing here and there. I take on the colors of each person I meet to some degree, temporarily of course.

A chameleon personality is the adjective I think would best describe the person I have become. It was lingering too long in its cocoon and will have to try its wings for a while. Then perhaps, only perhaps, I will have a specific identity. Actually, I am thoroughly enjoying my new wings. I do get weary if I fly too long or too far, but by the next morning I am rejuvenated and waiting for the next wind to blow me in whatever direction it is going.

Who am I? Is there a particular spot for me to land? If I am unattached, I soar. For most of my life I have been connected to someone I loved who needed me and therefore my flight was restrained. The freshness of my new life is exhilarating and yet there is a sadness of being released with no true goal.

I've always been a good navigator and if I just follow the course I am going I will probably reach the destination. I'm no longer the woman I was but I don't know if I'm the woman I is!

WAITING FOR GODOT AND OTHER STORIES

April 25, 1993

We're both waiting. Finian, our cat, and me. We're both waiting. He just came up for breakfast #2. Both small meals; he's no glutton. He's watching, washing and waiting. He glances up from his toilet and stares into the hallway. Where are you? Then he resumes his grooming. He is so very aware of your absence. Sometimes I think he is trying to comfort me in his cat-like ways. He sits near me when he is in the house much more often than was his custom. He comes over and sits in my lap several times in the evening when I'm watching television. All I have to say is "Finian, come over and talk to me."

He sleeps on the couch in the corner you occupied so much of your life. He is truly the only living creature that knew you as well as I did. We're both waiting. I know you are not returning. I think he knows too, but he hasn't given up hope yet. How I wish I did not feel this hopelessness. This despair, this grief which is beyond words, beyond tears.

I feel at times like a combination of the characters in the Wizard of Oz; the tin man who was looking for a heart, the scarecrow who was looking for a brain, and the lion who was looking for courage. I've always used the phrase "..follow the yellow brick road," as Finian is laying on the floor in the sunshine consumed by washing his beautiful fur, I sit in the chair and again plan to "...follow the yellow brick road."

I'm off to see the wizard (to be defined as whatever or whoever I encounter on my travels). As Dorothy said, "I'm not in Kansas anymore." I'm somewhere else, but I haven't identified it yet. Fortunately for me, just as Dorothy had her dog, Toto, I have my cat, Finian. You need a companion on your journey through life. Thanks for being my friend, Finian, it's just us two cats now.

"LIFE IS REAL, LIFE IS EARNEST AND THE GRAVE IS NOT ITS GOAL."

Henry W. Longfellow

April 26, 1993

"Tell me not in mournful numbers, life is but an empty dream and the soul is dead that slumbers and life is not what it seems."

Lines from a poem by Henry Wadsworth Longfellow, a poem I memorized for school way back when. I always loved to recite this poem. I didn't pay much attention to the words. I loved the rhythm. Now I think I'm ready for the words. At long last, the words are making their entrance into my awareness—not totally, just now and again.

I don't run from reality. I just don't embrace it. After all, if the words were really true, "life is but an empty dream," or true to me, I would have been defeated by life long ago. Sure, life is dream-like and much of it empty, but I believe mostly in the line "Life is not what it seems."

Life, as I know it and live it, is ever-changing like the weather , but it does have its seasons; not in the order of the seasons, i.e., summer, autumn, winter or spring. In life, one day may be "spring" and the next day a cold, cold winter, then onto an autumn of falling leaves and sadness, leaving sunny, warm summer behind.

Oh Henry Wadsworth Longfellow, you were some piece of work! You wrote elegantly, beautifully, and I'm glad my teacher made me memorize your poem. It has served me well. First, as the delight of the rhythm and the hum in the song of poetry and now and then the knowledge it imparts to us through verse. Thank you, Henry!

IT'S JUST THE GYPSY IN MY SOUL

April 27, 1993

Back to my songfest, my random ramblings on page and in life brings to the surface the "gypsy" within. I don't think the word has a singular definition. In my case, it is the restlessness, the semi-wildness that has always churned deep within me. The strong desire to see everything, go everywhere, talk to everyone and on and on it goes.

Who in the world wound me up so tight? My springs are unwinding, but I am a long way from running down. I can remember when I was very young, the urge to explore, to play, to engage in conversations with so many people, my friends and their parents. I never seemed to differentiate between the ages. Of course, I was mostly absorbed in school and playing, but not out of necessity, just the joy I felt at living. I was this very alive child that wanted to smell the new-cut grass and relish the scent of rain on the warm dirt in summer. I can remember picking up handfuls of dirt and bringing it close to my face to inhale the perfume the rain had brought forth from the soil.

On and on I went. There were the quiet years, with some people at some time. The other kids in school whom I felt threatened by, not physically. I could sense I was not in their frame of reference and receded into my studious mode, but after school, watch out world, I was back to the "gypsy" who danced, played and sung.

Time does pass and then there were the boy friends and the endless jobs. Three years of endless jobs! I counted once and I think I had twenty-one jobs in three years. Some I quit, some I was fired. I was always efficient, but the "gypsy" could not stand the strangulation of a mindless task of repetition. I went forth into a marriage. Ten years of a marriage, but the "gypsy" had no ground rules. She was loved and so she had no schedules as such, she could do pretty much what she desired and therefore, she thrived.

One day or week, or month, she realized her audience did not appreciate her art form and she felt neglected, unnecessary, and so she returned to the wild. Back to work, back to the routine. Even a gypsy needs to have money for the basics of life.

It was sad and it was joyful. Many admirers and the freedom of dancing to her own tune. Again, the marriage syndrome; she went unwillingly into her new habitat. But how could she refuse the total love, attention, praise that were heaped upon her by the man she married? How tantalizing deep love can be! There were moments she would strain at her unseen leash, but not even a gypsy can turn her back on love. She returned the love and for the most part seemed to put her gypsy tendencies aside. For the type of life she was required to live, to qualify for the immense love that was bestowed on her.

No one can turn their back on love. Life ends, but love lives on. The gypsy that is me is no longer confined to any particular time or place and slowly, she began dancing again. Sometimes at a maddening pace, sometimes a little more decorously.

"Gypsy, what do you plan to do now that you are being rejuvenated into the original 'you'?" I will dance, I will play and maybe, just maybe, I will love someone else again. Or maybe, just maybe I'll keep on dancing.

GETTING DOWN

April 28, 1993

Sometimes I feel or I know that my socializing, my running madly between stores and lunches is related to the panic that is under the surface, bubbling, smoldering, about to surface. I cannot afford or allow this panic to take shape and perhaps disfigure my persona. So I run. I talk, but the panic persists. It's not a true frightening panic. It is more a steady undercurrent that keeps me elevated on its back.

At times, especially lately, I just want to stop running, stop talking and lay back in the quiet shelter of myself. As soon as someone calls or some errand needs to be attended to, my constant companion, the inner panic, presents itself to follow me through the day. It is not unfriendly. It is not threatening. It just exists as a part of the day pushing me, pulling me and sitting beside me.

Each morning it is waiting for me when I awake. It eats breakfast with me, reads the paper and waits patiently until I take notice of its presence. It knows full well that sooner or later we'll be a team. We'll play the game of having fun and maybe at times we actually do, but it would be nice to replace panic with peace.

Maybe in time, maybe I'll enjoy the freneticism of panic. Maybe I need something between panic and peace, but I haven't the faintest clue or how to find whatever it is to slow me down, to feel mellow and yet not lose my enthusiasm. Living is a fine balance, like an acrobat walking on a wire. Equilibrium is achieved through practice and self confidence. I have a little of each, but not enough yet to walk the fine line that extends before me. I will try not to fall off. I will keep practicing and rest a little more.

We all need a time out. I have taken a few, but I think the time is coming to turn down the volume of life sounds and withdraw into a placid stream of silent introspection. Start feeling the warmth of the sun, enjoy the breeze on my face, sit quietly and listen, discover the taste of food eaten slowly and make plans to do something or go somewhere that will please your eyes, your ears and your soul.

ON THE ROAD AGAIN (THANKS, WILLIE NELSON)

April 30, 1993

I feel like a car that was put up on blocks and stored and kept under wraps or cover for the duration. I know when men went to war their families kept guard over this prized possession. When and if they returned home, this remarkable machine would be available to them and take them wherever they wanted to go.

I feel like the car. I have been garaged for many, many years. I have just opened the garage doors and looked at the remarkable machine that is me. I find that the engine or motor is still able to start. The interior is dusty, but that shouldn't be hard to take care of. The exterior is a little faded, but with a little polish it won't look bad. It's the inner workings that are the most important. The gears, the carburetor, the battery. They seem in good condition, but only time will tell how far the car will run or how well.

I am investing some time in recharging my battery. I am moving about to keep the gears more fluid. I'm not sure what a carburetor is. I have enough fuel and the tires look fine. It will be good to be out of storage and back on the road!

I'm looking forward to new horizons, different roads and a possible adventure around the bend. It wasn't bad being out of commission for so many years. I feel that I've perhaps saved the best for last. I will be able to breath on my own the rest of my life and it is truly an exhilarating release of pent-up energy!

After so many years in hibernation I will be able to truly appreciate the world around me. It is all new now and so I am off and running. I wish me "Bon Voyage"!

LONGTIME COMPANION

April 30, 1993

There is a fellow who sleeps with me most nights. He is very good looking and has sleek shiny dark hair. He is loving in an independent manly sort of way. He has been my live-in lover for almost twelve years which in these days are long-time relationships.

He doesn't snore and sleeps quietly not to disturb me. Sometimes in the early hours he arises, but does not wake me till almost seven o'clock in the morning. I have complained to him about this, but it seems to do no good. You know men! They just look at you and wonder why you don't get up to fix breakfast. He is not particularly demanding, but he does like to start the day on a full stomach.

Still, I do love him. He has so much grace and charm. He moves with slinky movements through the house further enchanting me. I cannot find words to reproach him even when his behavior becomes belligerent and tempestuous. It is nice to have a fellow around to feel his warmth and admiring looks.

His name, to clarify, this inhabitant of my abode, is Finian McLonergan. When he looks at me with his beautiful green eyes, I must admit, he is the handsomest cat I ever saw!

ONE OF THESE DAYS

May 2, 1993

This is one of these I-wish-I-was-dead days. I have had my share of these days, but I have hesitated to put it down on paper. It seems that by writing it down, a bare-faced statement, I might be courting disaster or someone will put a hex on me.

If you just feel like dying nothing will happen, but making the words come alive seem to have a different connotation. Nevertheless, I said it and I'm glad! Come what may, the words are out.

Today is also my mother's birthday. She would be one-hundred and one years old if she were alive, but she made it to ninety-four. So I guess if we have to die, ninety-four is not too bad. I don't know why we have to die. I just know that we do and I really do not care for death one little bit.

I have control over many things in my life. Weather and death are beyond my control. The weather is okay. I love weather. I love rain, I love thunder, I love all the seasons. Death on the other hand, has no redeeming feature. It is just the end of something or someone who was special. Even flowers die and of course, cats and dogs. The sadness of death invades our lives continually in one form or another. It mostly seems like a very distant relative whom you've never met and will probably never meet. Then, lo and behold, it is standing at your door—I'm here—you are totally unprepared for guests, especially this unwelcome guest.

You handle the arrival rather calmly, unbelievingly, but since it has entered your space, there is really nothing to do, but accommodate it to the best of your ability. I gave it respect, surrounded it with all the comforts of my home. I didn't rant and rave and question its arrival.

Looking back, overall I handled it graciously and with much dignity. Considering it was a most unwanted guest, I am proud of myself in retrospect. Now that I have met death and it has entered my life, I would wish it move away for a while and then I won't have any more of these I-wish-I-were-dead days. Its presence still pervades my house and I would like to have more of I'm-glad-I-am-alive days. I guess death will move away in its own sweet time, but I would like to give it a push!

PAY DIRT

May 3, 1993

I have friends in high places. I don't know if I have written about this before. If I did, it will be Act II, Scene I. I am not aware of these friends or high places, but every so often something happens to alert me to the fact.

Something particularly pleasant happens to me that comes out of the blue; no more expected and completely unsolicited. Sure, I suppose I send out vibrations of one kind or another and I suppose what I am sending out hits an unseen nerve in someone who sends back messages in the form of a positive, warm response. Even inanimate objects have been responsive in that I can find the something I was looking for and even not knowing I was.

There are many periods of my day. Just the garden variety times we all live with, but if I reach deep within me in my solitude, I find the garden has many plants. I can pick from a tree or reach down and pull up a fresh idea. The humans in my life grow on the trees. They stand erect. They are proud and some have not yet fully ripened. There are so many varieties and so many waiting to be picked. By picked I mean talked to, listened to, encouraged and most of the times left to resume their growing.

On the other hand the garden of ideas is mine exclusively. I can plant, I can harvest. I am not a very good gardener yet, but I do see a few buds trying to open and if I nurture them I might even be successful enough to wake one day and see something in full bloom. I procrastinate about my efforts. I've never tried or wanted to have a garden. My life was my garden, but I lost the man in charge. Now it is my turn to take charge and see what I can grow.

"Mary, Mary quite contrary, how does your garden grow?"
"With tinker bells and big sea shells and maidens all in a row."

I'll have to look up this nursery rhyme. I'm sure I've got it wrong, but with apologies to Mary, I'd like to see what I will produce "all in a row."

BRINGING IN THE SHEAVES

May 5, 1993

I'm learning to hang back. This, to be translated, as not frenetically going here and there; starting conversation with whomever happens to be in my line of vision. I've been many heres and theres and have had many conversations. I think like a farmer who distributes seeds through the fields after preparing his farm for the new crop. I have been throwing out seeds (food for thought or invitations to be accepted), I will now have to wait and see what my efforts bring forth.

I have already began to reap some rewards for my haphazard maneuverings in a desperate move to start a new life, like a new crop. I had no idea in the beginning of what I could or could not achieve by my disjointed alliances, but now it is beginning to take shape. It is almost like I was in an embryonic stage and have developed eyes, arms and legs enabling me to see more, feel more and go more. I have not yet totally utilized this new creature inside me.

I am still mostly what I am and will always be, but to start a new life, I instinctively must have known that another part of my persona has to emerge in order to live a more complete life. As follows, new people, new experiences are necessary for a new life. It's impossible to remain status quo or you just deteriorate into a somnambulist state which might be comfortable, but stagnant. The embryo within me is much too restless and I followed its lead and I have developed and will go on developing until death do us part.

MIDNIGHT WORLD

May 6, 1993

I had a dream last night. I have a lot of dreams and mostly I don't remember them by the time I awake. This time I had a dream, a very real dream. I dreamt I was asleep and when I awoke it was very dark outside. I looked at the clock and it was seven o'clock in the morning I thought. I guess it is cloudy and I went to the window, but the sky was black. It was a midnight sky. The passing of the day did not change the color of the sky. I was spending my day in the blackness of night. It was not frightening. It just seemed to be a natural phenomenon of nature. Perhaps, when I awake tomorrow it will no longer be night, but for now, I will live in a midnight world.

And then, you appeared. I said, "You are dead!"

You answered, "Do I look like I'm dead?"

"No," I replied.

You said, "I'm looking for my clothes and shoes. I can't find them."

I said, "I gave away most of your things after you died."

You became angry and looked at me with bewilderment. I said, "I still have most of your pants and jackets."

You then replied, "What about shirts, underwear, socks and shoes?"

I was very apologetic and said it in a timid voice, "I thought you were dead." It seemed so very real, I felt so very bad that I had given away your clothes. I was beside myself with remorse. I think I remember saying, "We could go to the store and buy what you need."

Then the dream faded and I was back again in my midnight world, alone.

ONCE UPON A TIME

May 7, 1993

I remember, I loved to dance. I still do, but I haven't in a long time. When I was about seven and we moved to the wrong side of the tracks, my career as a dancer became a reality. My parents had purchased a store with two rooms adjoining, a tourist court with six separate cabins and a tabernacle in the back of a huge lot where church services were held every Sunday. When the church people had a revival, I think they came in every evening for a week.

But to get back to my dancing debut. Three or four elderly or disabled men were allowed to move into our cabins. I think the city welfare paid their rent and gave them money for food. I somehow discovered that they were an eager audience. I would knock on each door and say, "I'll dance for a penny!" They always smiled and said, "Yes," and gave me a penny. I did some sort of tap dance and sang Shoe Shine Boy:

"Shoe shine boy, you work hard all day,
Shoe shine boy got no time to play.
Every penny helps a lot,
So shine, shine, shoe shine boy!"

I don't know why or when they left, but as long as I was performing, I loved the limelight. The penny was incidental. Oh, how I loved an audience!

Years later when I was about ten or eleven years old I would go on the stage in the tabernacle. It was a wide wooden stage, upon which rested a huge blackboard. The preacher would write scriptures on it each Sunday to explain God and the devil to the churchgoers, but in the middle of the week it was my theater.

I had come a long way. I could now tap, sort of, and sing "Anchor's away my boy, anchors away," and go dancing from one side of the stage to the other. I needed an audience. The only children I knew who would sit passively on the wooden benches were Mary, Martha and Joseph Merrill, the triplets from next door. Their parents were Christian Scientists and didn't believe in doctors. There were a lot of Merrill children. The oldest, Van, Samuel, Daniel, David, Paul and Mary, Martha and Joseph. They would sit quietly on the benches, looking up at me stolidly while I sang and danced.

They were totally under my spell. They did whatever I told them to do. Once I made make-believe sodas out of soapy water and crushed grass and told them they were lime sodas and they even drank a little until I stopped them. I could not be that cruel. Even then I realized that power is not to be taken lightly and not to be abused.

FRINGE BENEFIT

May 9, 1993

I feel I'm full of words, phrases, and thoughts. There is no cohesiveness to my words and thoughts, but maybe in time I can sit back and see what I have given birth to. At this point there is no form, just a sensation of a beginning of new life.

I realized early this morning that I have been a *fringe benefit* in the partnerships I have been involved in. Starting with my parents; I was the studious, cheerful and mostly obedient child. Then on to teens and adulthood. My mother lived vicariously through me—my boy friends, my parties, my sense of fun and even my restlessness.

During this time, my father sat back and did not want to take part. I was much too much for him. In retrospect, he was an intelligent, sensitive, inhibited man who found great difficulty in facing the world. Laughter was something foreign to him. Every now and then a brief chuckle, but he never allowed himself the laughter I was so involved with.

On the other hand, my mother loved to smile and I was truly her *fringe benefit.* She never stifled my joy—she reveled in it. She always seemed to blossom while we were together.

And then there were two. I married early and began the duties of a wife. I don't think Bob wanted the kind of wife I was. I was useful, true, but I really don't know what he would have wanted in a wife besides the "mother of his children"; that is what he told me he wanted. Neither of us were capable of being parents. I was neat, I cooked more or less and I became involved with his aunt and uncle and retarded sister.

I helped his aunt achieve her long-time dream. After forty years I helped her become an American citizen. I taught Ethel, his retarded sister, to play cards whereupon she won every time. I helped his uncle on Fridays in his grocery store when it was crowded with men cashing checks.

I think I loved Bob. I don't know, but he was tall and loved to dance. When he included me in his plans, life was pleasurable. I was only a *fringe benefit* though. When we divorced, he said, "How am I going to find my socks and underwear?" I was reduced to the status of a competent housekeeper.

Then I met the Man. The Man, Mel. He could laugh, but not too often. He could play if I started the game. His greatest virtue was giving. He gave totally. He gave compassion, he gave love, he gave commitment. He had to be in charge and needed the role of head of household. He needed to be consulted in all things. I gladly handed over my life to him.

He was my benevolent tyrant. I only had the responsibility of carrying out his wishes, but since he was so eager to please me his wishes were to my benefit. He was my protector, he was my knight in shining armor. I was his *fringe benefit.* I again took up the duties of a wife; the cleaning and some cooking. I listened to his words, his frustrations and the dreams he hadn't realized. I gave him the solace he needed. I gave him the love or as much of the love he required.

I always kept some of me to myself. There has always been a guarded corner of my life that is my exclusive property. I can retreat there when necessary and no one is the wiser or hurt by my seclusion. I was his *fringe benefit.*

Life did not offer him the substantial awards he deserved. His sensitive soul was badly bruised beginning with his childhood. Inside this strong, courageous man there lived a frightened, fragile child. I don't think I ever gave the child the warmth and love it needed. I tried, but it always retreated into some hidden crevice of the man. I would have liked so much to have put my arms around the child and tell him he was special, he was good, he was so worthwhile, but even good intentions don't always help unless the child is allowed the freedom to emerge.

I did so many things. Some frivolous, some with great effort. I tried, oh how I tried, to be an asset to this unusual man. The world will never see his likes again. The world did not see or know this man. I did and it has given me great strength and knowledge. I have been an appreciative student and now I hope for the rest of my life, I will turn to him who is no longer here and heed his advice.

There are so many volumes in my memory bank. I just have to open the right book for the right answer. Being a *fringe benefit* is actually a pretty good thing; I am now reaping the benefits of being part of so many lives.

YOU RASCAL, YOU!

May 10, 1993

I'm trying to write with the sound of music in the background. I've never done this before. It seems to keep disrupting my thoughts and it probably does, but I'll see what comes out my fingertips with a musical accompaniment. I mostly feel like getting up and dancing. I can't sing, but music does stir my body and feet.

I woke up this morning with the song reeling through my brain: "I'll be glad when you're dead, you rascal you." I can't think of the rest of the lyrics, but if I remember I'll put an addendum to these scribblings.

We had talked about death now and then. You know, the usual I-wish-I-was-dead or You'll-probably-miss-me-when-I-die or I-wish-I-was-never-born. Oddly enough we've all had these thoughts and even if we didn't verbalize them, they are lying around in our subconscious. After all, since death is inevitable, it is a part of our very essence to be aware of our dying, or the dying of others.

It seems so very, very far from being reality that even if someone we know dies, we don't accept the finality of death. We talk of the one who died like they have moved to a distant country and actually expect to see them again some day. We use the words 'they died long ago or recently', but they are just words. No one we know or knew ever dies. I think all of us somehow meld and become part of each other. That is all of us who care and took the time to know our most precious friends and family.

CHASING MY TAIL

May 12, 1993

I've literally been chasing my tail. We've all seen kittens and puppies look out the corner of their eyes and they begin slowly and then swiftly. Before they know it, they are in a frenzy to capture that illusive object just beyond their reach.

I don't know when I became aware of my chase for the illusive object just beyond my reach, but I do know why. When your life is reduced to only yourself, your need to reach out is magnified to the point where at some point you realize you are never going to catch or define what is behind you. It isn't even necessary to try. You have to relax, not totally, and push your button on your *cruise control* to *resume*. Whatever speed you set for yourself can be accelerated if desired or kept at your own internal speed limit or just slowed down to *coast.*

I need to keep within my limits. At this time my destination is unknown except, of course, the final destination. I'm missing my insight. I'm missing self-revelation. Now that I have the time to do a little research, I need to reduce my speed and spend more time on introspection.

I think I have ambivalent feelings toward introspection. I feel I will find too little. Do I stop running in circles? Do I try to focus on some evanescent talent that has evaded me these may years? Do I keep on *stomping at the Savoy?* My euphemism for letting the flotsam and jetsam of my life direct me and refuse to take charge of my own destiny. This whole treatise sounds to me like the 'mumbo, jumbo' of, as Shakespeare wrote "...the sound and fury, signifying nothing."

If it be so, let my "sound and fury" signify some small echo to be heard by whoever can hear. *Attention must be paid!*

THROUGH A GLASS DARKLY

May 12, 1993

I'm trying to get it right. I'm trying to understand our relationship. I'm trying to analyze how two people live together for many years. What makes it right? Where do you go wrong? How is a long-term marriage possible or does it at times become impossible?

All of the above is true, but it is only the tip of the iceberg of what was there and the definition of love and marriage is much too complex. No two marriages are alike. Tonight I realized one of our basic problems. We were too often separated by a wall of pain. Physical pain for the most part. We both had much physical pain and many surgeries. We both endured severe and intense discomfort so we could not share enough of the good times that we were entitled to and deserved.

My wall of pain did not stop my love for you and your compassion was beyond the call of duty. Much of our lives, I laughed through pain and I functioned through pain. But pain clouds the mind and I most probably inadvertently neglected some special need you must have had. I tried, I know I tried, but no one who lives with pain can be complete and totally selfless.

I became angry and frustrated at the obstinacy of the division between us and you became weakened by its persistence and neither of us could reach each other and touch. We were reduced to looking through the glass of pain and refusing to acknowledge that all we had left were soft glances, gentle touches and a deep yearning to be closer to each other.

In some very strange way, I feel closer to you now. I know you are gone, but so is the wall of pain and my memories of all you were will live with me forever.

WHERE DO I GO FROM HERE?

May 14, 1993

Everybody I meet seems to be hiding. We talk together, we eat together, but I feel and know there is a person behind the face that I haven't met, and don't know and probably never will. It's a strange, strange world I've entered. Its is filled with people who are polite and gracious and well mannered. But who are they?

The persona that is revealed to me is no revelation at all. It is a surface road over a foundation of gravel, stone or a myriad of uneven surfaces that are the sum total of what we become in an effort to be acceptable to the world around us.

I have an irresistible desire to tear away the masks and find the reality that exists in everyone. I do not want to be cruel, but why is it necessary for me to cajole and humor each and every one I meet to get to know who is hiding behind their screens? My inordinate desire for this knowledge is beyond curiosity. I need to know. Perhaps because I am searching for myself and each time I catch a glimpse through the cracks in their armor, I become a more knowing and caring person myself!

I have lived on the fringe all my life, but in protective custody. I don't know how much I want to leave the safety of my self-imposed barriers. The safety is a strong factor in not venturing too far, but mostly by spending more time in contemplative repose, I will truly find my road for future travels.

Each of us is a map. A map with the original state of being and then the highlights of our life are in heavier type while the everyday garden varieties are in smaller, lesser print. There have been mountains, valleys, plains for all of us and though not the same, our roads do merge here and there.

What I am looking for in all the people I am meeting now is our common denominator: where our roads met somewhere, at some time. What we did at those cross sections and how did we feel? Were we happy, sad or somewhere in between? I am my own cartographer and though I can remember much of my journey through life up to this point, I need to know if life was worth the trip and if it was , what now or is now just that now?

STILL LAUGHING

May 14, 1993

I know a few people who are like light switches. When I talk to them it becomes lighter and the glow that surrounds me is warm and friendly. My words and thoughts flow from my mind through my lips and disappear into the air. They turn on the light of my mind. The conversation does not have to be psychological or philosophical in nature. It is some sort of magic that occurs when certain people free-fall with you. We bounce up and down on the trampoline of mundane subjects and we empathize with each other's discomforts, but mostly we laugh. We enjoy the ridiculousness that pervades our lives.

Life to be perfectly honest is silly much of the time. Starting from the time you get up in the morning and having breakfast, to rushing through your day, through being utterly foolish if you view yourself as I do. I find I'm very funny. Not funny 'hah-hah,' just sort of bemused by life and even death. I don't know where or how I arrived at the humor I seem to find in most things.

I remember when the doctor told my husband who was in need of a serious operation which he was apprehensive about. The good doctor said, "Well, if you are not satisfied with your quality of life, the operation should be considered."

My husband was very serious about his quality of life and chose the surgery. He died. All that has run through my mind all day is, "The quality of life is death."

How silly, how totally foolish! What is the quality of life? How do we measure quality and to go further, how do we judge life? In his case, the quality of his life was his death. He chose to gamble and lost. We all lose in the end, but we also lose all along the way.

Why is death funny or silly? I don't know except it makes no sense to me, ergo no sense is nonsense and so again humor saves my day! Maybe I'm not funny at all, but it keeps me sane and open to the rest of the days. If humor is my strength, so be it. Bless laughter; tears of laughter are still tears!

PALACE OF SWEETS (MEMORIES ARE MADE OF THIS)

May 14, 1993

I remember the Palace of Sweets. It was a marble floored, marbled counter, ice cream parlor in the Texas town I was born and grew up in. It had large ceiling fans that whirred through the hot days of summer. Large white birds cooling us while we sat in our ice cream chairs, wrought iron chairs painted white, and glass tables with frosted glass rounds. For the smaller children, a smaller table and chairs identical to the adult size. What a special place!

I loved the ice cream sodas. I never had a sundae; occasionally a banana split, but they were expensive with the sliced bananas, three flavors of rounded scoops of ice cream, whipped cream and a sprinkle of nuts and a cherry. They were good, but they weren't friendly like sodas. The sodas stood tall and you drank from a straw for a long, long time until the ice cream was almost melted. With my last breath I pulled on the straw and made a slurpy sound which made me feel a bit wicked for being noisy in public.

I remember the special day at the Palace of Sweets. It was Sunday and I was almost twelve years old. I was confirmed that day in a long, white organza dress. My mother and father took me for a soda afterwards and I felt so elated! I was confirmed. I was wearing a beautiful, long dress. I was escorted by my mother and father. We then went to the best and most expensive movie theater in town. Twenty-five cents; this was 1936. We saw the movie "San Francisco" starring Jeanette McDonald and Nelson Eddy. I still remember my delight at this whole glorious day. Little did I know I would move to San Francisco and so I did.

I am still delighted by San Francisco. The Palace of Sweets is long gone and so are my parents and so are Jeanette McDonald and Nelson Eddy. I have a picture of me in my white confirmation dress. And I still live in San Francisco.

THE UNSPOKEN

May 15, 1993

Finian just came up the stairs. He looked at me and I knew he wanted to know, "Where's the boss?"

I said, "The boss is gone, you're the boss now. You're the head of the household with your white chin." He gave me a grave look and sprawled leisurely and gracefully on the floor near me. He is quite capable of being "head of household." I do consult him and I know his responses without words. When you've lived together for many years, you don't need too many words to convey your feelings.

I need words though, and I can still feel them all day when I'm alone, bubbling and churning their way to reach the surface and exit through my mouth. Since there is no one to hear them, they are all impacted somewhere in the middle of my chest. I can talk and talk to other people, but the important words that were meant for the one I had lived with and loved for many years are still laying undisturbed inside me. Maybe I will never be able to voice my true feelings again or possibly some of them to someone someday. But not yet.

I have started a whole new life. A life of silence. I still talk, but it is more like a stranger talking than the person I think I am.

The only living thing I can still truly talk to is Finian. We are completely in sync. We feel each other's emotions. We can relax together. We can be sad together. We can delight in the warmth of the sunshine and of course, we sleep together. He is my "Main Man" now. He's not too demanding, but he does wake me up too early with his incessant meowing. Finally I reluctantly crawl out of bed and serve the master his breakfast whereupon he retreats to the outside down the stairs through the garage and laundry room, down the stairs across the deck into the yard to perform his daily toilet. Then sometimes, like today, he returns within the hour to lay near me and groom himself, but mostly meditates.

I don't know about this cat and his eating habits, but I don't question it! I give him the food he likes in whatever manner he likes and while I in turn do the same thing with my meals. This style, meaning Finian and myself, might seem a bit eccentric to others, but I do believe in comfort for the soul, be it in the form of food, clothing, entertainment, I do believe in comfort. Just file me in the comfort zone, me and Finian.

IS ANYONE LISTENING?

May 15, 1993

When voices were invented, I got one of the first ones. I started talking early and have been on a roll ever since. I've talked sense and nonsense. I've talked to hear the sound and to hear the fury. Oh yes, I have a voice, but for the most part people don't listen. They sit and nod their heads and wait for a break in your conversation to begin their own verbal sounds and then you realize that your voice is rarely heard. Your words are taken literally if at all and nobody, and I mean nobody, knows what you are saying. You are trying to impart and share your life, your dreams, your adventures and apparently you are the only one who is listening.

Then you decide to stop talking, temporarily at least. Almost every subject is of interest to me, but the longer you live the more you realize that people live in their own boxes or boundaries and can't move beyond their borders or containers.

I listen a lot. I am curious and always eager to hear. I live on a 'need to know' basis, but until I find that rare someone or someones, I will have to accept the fact that my words are falling on deaf ears. It's just that most people can't hear too many sounds. The world as a whole is hearing impaired. After all, if most of us could hear, we wouldn't have wars, we would feel more compassion, we could truly be the better for it.

I know in my time, which is this time, that "tilting at windmills" is not only the Don Quixote persona. All of us dreamers who walk the earth want so much to know everyone, touch everything, see everything and on it goes.

Dreamers of the world unite! We are special! Nothing can truly diminish our dreams. We are isolated, but not alone. We must try to impart some of what we feel to others and if it doesn't happen, so be it. We are what we are. So begins the summer of content or discontent depending entirely on our own meteorological knowledge.

THE OUTSIDER

May 18, 1993

I'm trying to find my niche. No matter where I go or whom I'm with, I feel like a round peg in a square hole or vice versa. I have met many friendly and kind people, or so it seems, but when I look around I only see how sad we all are. We are all older and getting much older and everyone seems to be grasping at some lifeline, be it an intellectual discussion, raising money for a noble cause or both of the above.

I am no better or worse than these folks, but I don't fit. I've never fit anywhere with hardly anyone. I always feel removed from the scene and though I listen and talk and nod and smile, I am no more a part of the group than if I was an alien being who just landed on this planet.

I don't really know where to go from here. I do like the social part, but I really don't want to be involved beyond that. For whatever reason, I am what I am whatever that is and I am an alien in a strange land. Maybe just because I've been turned loose upon the earth at this late date in my development, I don't assimilate well.

I don't know whether anyone has noticed that I am an alien being, but I know. I seem to want to smile at my own frailties and really wonder what my purpose is here on this earth. Others seem to have accepted their lot or so it seems. I, on the other hand, accept nothing and will continue to search and perhaps be lucky to find what slot suits me and be able to come to terms with my own estrangement.

SLIGHTLY ASKEW

May 19, 1993

I just dialed a number and a very nice voice answered and told me I was 'off by a digit'. I realized that that is the story of my life. I've always been off by a digit. If I try I can usually get the right number or move efficiently in the right direction and get the thing done, but mostly I'm 'off by a digit'.

This is not a bad thing. Actually, it keeps me on my toes and when you go dancing through life (figuratively, of course) it is good to stub your toes now and then. It is good to be aware that mistakes have to be made, bad judgment calls have to be recognized, frivolous wanderings have to be reduced to a more manageable area.

Most of all, being 'off by a digit' gives you the opportunity to laugh at adversities, not be apologetic for stumbling and the freedom to be human or in my case an imperfect being who has no desire to be perfect. Just 'off by a digit.'

"WHAT'LL I DO?"

May 22, 1993

It seems that my life lately has become a series of song titles. For instance, "What'll I do when you are far away, what'll I do?" credit to songwriter, Irving Berlin. I know what I'm doing more or less, but then the melody insinuates itself into my mind and I find myself asking "What'll I do?" Berlin also wrote "All alone, I'm so all alone...," and that goes without saying or humming. I know I'm all alone. "All I do is dream of you the whole night through."

Actually, I don't dream of you the whole night through. You have most of the twenty-four hours of the day. It's not a dream, you are with me twenty-four hours. Sometimes I feel that you are quietly sitting in the other room when I'm talking on the phone. But once I stop, I remember you day and night.

You are still sitting quietly in the other room. No longer visible, but you are there, absolutely there. Every song brings back a memory or memories. We are a country of songs of emotion. At this point I will close my repertoire with "I'm bidin' my time, that's the kind of girl I am, hum, hum, I'm bidin' my time."

I'M OUT!

May 25, 1993

Who let me out of my cage? Who put me in there in the first place? Was I born in a cage? Probably.

I suppose we all are; big cages, little cages, but we are caught up in some limited space depending upon our own character and those around us. Depending on where we were born and our financial status, depending upon our parents and what freedom they allowed, but the most important thing of all, is the freedom we allow ourselves.

I have lived all my life in a series of cages. Most of them have been comfortable and I haven't felt the need to wander around in the outside jungle. And all of a sudden, my cage door has swung open. Actually the door is gone and I am wandering through the jungle of life and experiencing the smells and tastes of total freedom. There are no restraints upon me; no demands, no time limits and sometimes I feel sad because it seems that no one cares. It's not easy to accept this total release. I think I can understand why people who have spent years in prison find it hard to adjust to life on the outside.

I am moving about freely, but I find this exhilarating and tiring. I find myself expressing opinions and thoughts that I never knew I had. I have talked and spent time with people I never would have met. I feel at times I'm spinning out of control, but I still have my safe place, my haven, my home which always welcomes me and offers me solace.

In my safe place, I am surrounded by all the memories of my life and the warmth permeates my soul. I've never felt so needed by so many and yet, though I still need all of them, my need has yet to be satisfied. I am still thirsty for the springs needed to replenish my soul.

Meanwhile, out of my cage, I go hither and yon and I doubt very seriously that I will be able to stand confinement again. I will have to learn to live more peaceably in the jungle. It will be good; life will be good and as I said today to someone, "I can stop running and coast the rest of my way through life."

COMMONSENSICAL

May 27, 1993

So many people are caught up in therapy. I am not writing this to judge them or whether or not the expense and time in therapy is worthwhile. I do not know people's deepest feelings, lack of self worth, fears and etc., but it seems to me that life is a "back to basics"; the world is full of "dysfunctional families," of people who probably were not *nurtured* or *bonded* with their parents or siblings. The *dysfunctional* _____ *inner child* is probably contained in all our psyches.

But why bother going back? Why not turn around and go forward? Are so many people frozen in time that it is necessary to live again, to return to the womb and start over? To actualize whatever was missing and to establish a more solid base, i.e., a sense of self to become more viable, self-confident, and happier in order to pursue life.

Wow! How lucky I am! I have a life! I feel good about myself! I have fears, but I confront them. I have doubts, but if I can't solve a problem, I dismiss it and move forward. I refuse to become sealed in a chamber of horrors (lack of self worth, fear of failure, restless ennui). I must have bonded and been nurtured, but I don't think that is the whole answer.

I was blessed with the commonsensical. I could laugh easily. Life was never a threat. Mistakes were never earth shattering and mostly I was very forgiving of myself and others. I reacted and acted, not always wisely, but well enough to go charging forward, stalling at times, stumbling here and there, but never retreating.

Onward, onward, she goes and where she stops? Nobody knows.

Oh, how lucky I am! My dysfunctional family obviously functioned well enough for me and my parents who had many, many barriers to confront and cross obviously nurtured me enough.

I needed to develop self. I needed to plant my own roots and grow my own person. I needed the independence to be me and whatever love that was distributed through my development was subtle and not suffocating. How lucky my inner child grew up!

BEWITCHED, BOTHERED, AND BEWILDERED

May 30, 1993

There I was, riding public transportation on my way to the great downtown to see a musical. As I boarded this local train, I was immediately struck by my fellow travelers. All sizes and colors and totally unresponsive to each other and each living in his, her, or their own orbit. One blond woman, forty-ish, stood swaying with the movement of the train. Slim, dressed in an assortment of garments, blue corduroy pants, gold blouse, layered with an orange vest, holding a blue denim jacket and a huge straw purse from which she pulled out a bent blue pencil, presumably of rubber-like material, with yellow leaves and a rose attached to the top with smaller green leaves which tumbled and shook as she scribbled something down on a yellow note pad.

The rose on top of the pen jiggled and shook and seem to be precariously attached to the top of the pencil. She finished, put everything back in her bag. She wore sandals with wide leather straps encasing her ankles. Long multi-colored glass earrings dangled from her ears and as she departed the train, I wondered what planet she was from and to what other worldly place was her destination.

All around me were aliens. Creatures from other worlds, some earth bound, some obviously beyond the pale. As I, too, departed the train, I entered another foreign world. Seething with color and clamor, the Powell Street estuary was disturbing and frightening. Numbers of alienated creatures who covered the sidewalks. No one, or hardly anyone, looked like the people I know or remember. I feel I entered into a dysfunctional world and I scurry past so as not to have their vibrations leave their mark on me.

As I enter the play, the world of music, I am enchanted, delighted and nostalgic. That was my world. The world of love and fun, the world of dance and longing, but it was real. My world was real. My world is still real, but too many of the population have moved into their own twilight zone and it is a world of darkness, pessimism and the acceptance of unreality. The world of drugs, street people, hustlers, neo-bohemians and indifferent social mores.

I am so glad I got to spend most of my life with warmth and love, with imagination and optimism. How sad that the world has evolved to the lowest common denominator. How sad.

MY FIRST MEMORIAL DAY

Memorial Day—May 30, 1993

I have to put this down on paper while it is still fresh in my mind. I drove to Golden Gate National Cemetery today. This is my first Memorial Day visit to the grave. As I drive in, I was overcome with awe and consummate sadness at the American flags lining the entrance and all the roads. As I gazed through dampened eyes, I saw over one-hundred-twenty-seven-thousand small American flags fluttering in the breeze in front of all the markers with all the names of all the men and women who served our country.

I was overwhelmed as I drove slowly to the grave that belonged to me. No words could possibly express my sadness and my wonder at the enormity of the thousands of flags waving happily in front of thousands of graves. I reached the grave with my own personal flag, but they had already placed one there. So I just placed it in an empty space so it, too, could stand proudly among the others. I added flowers to the vase, a mixture of white, red and crimson colors adorning the resting place.

I said a short prayer and looked upwards at the billowing clouds and watched the roaring planes depart overhead from the nearby airport. The planes have no respect for all you brave men and women. They just go busily about their way, flying here and there, depositing their human cargo.

All of you in the garden of flags, in the city of stones, have taken your last trip. Your voyages are over. You no longer need to pack or plan. You no longer have to anxiously await another plane or another anything. I found it so hard to leave this city of the noble dead. I found it so hard to leave. Only the name stamped so boldly on the marble slab is all that is left for me to stand near.

Eternity is yours now. I am waiting my turn. Please God, if there is a God, let us be together! I, too, want to lay beneath a fluttering flag. The breeze brushes my face. I felt it touching me gently, oh so gently. How lucky, how very lucky I have been to share my life and so many years with someone so loving and have been cherished by someone so noble! Thank you, God! Thank you!

I am overcome. I am truly undone by the enormity of these many graves and most especially by yours. Would that I not have lived to see you dead? The choice was not mine to make.

LOOK TO THE RAINBOW

June 5, 1993

As I was about to go to sleep I told my cat, Finian, you are my inspiration. I have to try and make sense of what has been rattling around in my mind these many years. I have a fertile mind. I have the seeds, but I have to water them if they are to grow. What my crop will be, remains to be seen, but there is a variety of plants and blossoms to be brought forward if I take the time to nourish them.

I've ignored the signals. I've ignored the flashes of ideas, thoughts, and various and sundry stirrings. Life has been a long and demanding partner and now that I'm unhitched from my wagon, there is no excuse for not letting my roaming mind and imagination have its day. It will be interesting and perhaps soothe the restlessness which has haunted me my whole life.

I've needed an outlet besides the usual chores of life and the talking and the nothingness that makes up my days. I have always refused to acknowledge the meaningless of so many days, months of my life. I let the time go by and I sat idly by and pulled myself inside out so that I wouldn't feel the time running on.

Do I have energy to try and produce something? Am I too lazy and will I let inertia overtake me and hold my hand in silent comfort? Will I follow the rainbow and try to find my pot of gold? I seem to see its glimmer in the far, far distance. I would hope I would follow the rainbow. Finian did and found happiness!

JUST WON TON

June 7, 1993

I went out and ate Chinese food,
and talked of this and that.
I went out and ate Chinese food,
and went back to my cat.

My perspective, it is faulty.
My judgment, it is flaky.
I think I know and then I don't .
My world right now is shaky.

I want to go, but don't know where.
I've stood and fought the good fight.
But now that life is sinking in,
I don't know if I can write.

What do I have to say
and why should anyone listen?
Words, more words, but only
Jewels and gold and gems do glisten

Do I have the ability to shine?
Do I have the ability to glow?
I guess I'll have to try;
seems the only way to know.

I went out and ate Chinese food
and got a fortune cookie.
The script upon the paper said,
"You only find by 'lookie'."

Confucius says, "Only go around once."
"Don't be afraid to be a dunce."
"Don't be afraid to make mistake."
"Brave people; chances take."

MY ROCKY ROAD

June 9, 1993

The malingering, piteous soul;
the mewling of self pity.
No ears to hear my wails, no audience needed for my travails
Alone, alone I twist inside.
I know exactly how you died.
I couldn't stop and hold you longer.
Death was a bully and much stronger.
I watched you die, I watched you leave.
You kept saying, "Stay, stay."
I didn't move, I didn't leave, I didn't even pray.
Nor could I stop the time of day.
Now I am angry, I don't know why.
Maybe it's because I cannot cry.
My soul is crying, it's in despair!
My eyes are dry and that's not fair!
I need to fill a well with tears.
I need to verbalize my fears.

ONCE UPON A MIDNIGHT WEARY, WHILE I PONDERED

June 9, 1993

Looking back today was a very strange day. I met with a literary group discussing a book about past history. I wanted to say what about now and what is happening today. I know the phrase "..those that don't know the mistakes of the past and have not learned from them are doomed to repeat them." True, but there were so many mistakes and history repeats itself with different players.

I feel we should just try to base our thoughts and our beliefs on our own pasts. We all have different pasts; sociologically, financially and philosophically. We only have so much time to interact and we must utilize our personal experiences.

As I have been told, I act or react immediately to a situation. While someone else is mulling over a problem, I've moved ahead to the next one. My decisions or actions are not necessarily correct, but when I think, I am in a hurry. I always have felt the winds of time blowing at my back and I must hurry my pace to keep up and keep ahead. I know somewhere I will be swept away and the thinking and doing will be done.

Again I say, today was a strange day. Ladies sitting and discussing in a lovely house surrounded by pictures, couches, chairs, Japanese prints, floral bedspreads, white glistening kitchen, pastels and brilliants. But there it was; the dining table fully set with lovely china (the plates, saucers, cups, the crystal goblets, silver spoons, the knives and forks). There it stood, stately and elegant.

I found by questioning my hostess there were no guests, nor none invited or expected. She had set the table so very formally on the day after her husband died two years ago. Two years the table sat waiting for a specter at the feast. The table itself was long and seemed rough hewn and painted a soft pastel. A table waiting. This was set by the woman who never sleeps.

Again, I say this was a strange day. Her life is filled with sons who care, but her early life was filled with despair. Now that she's alone and has no wall to lean on, the past, the distant past, has crept back in her life and kept her from facing tomorrow, and has imprisoned her in the rejection she grew up with and is keeping her captive.

I find myself feeling so well. I, too, don't get all that much sleep and I, too, cannot weep. But I am well. I can move forward. There are no demons in my past and those that are I have put in their place long ago. I was lucky. I set no table for my lost love. He gave too much love. My shrine to him is the strength he imparted to me.

Someday I'll sleep. Someday I'll weep and what will come to pass is that I will build on the foundation we built together. He showed me how to use the tools and I will use them well. I need more time to grieve. I will give myself more time. I will give myself whatever I need to continue my wellness.

In retrospect and by observing others, I find I am doing great. A dash of sadness, a sprinkle of depression and a dollop of fatigue. An easy recipe to prepare and put aside. The main course of my life is yet to be determined or defined. I am well and I am strong and I must remember to keep my reserves intact and not get caught up in others' nightmares. I am much too susceptible and will have to be on guard. I do care for all, but I must care the most for myself. Self preservation, remember my name.

THANK YOU

June 10, 1993

I guess life will have been worthwhile if we have had our fifteen minutes of fame. The renowned quote from the late Andy Warhol. As I sit here reminiscing, I try to remember the fifteen minutes each person I have known has made memorable to me. Each and every one I've known has achieved fame, some for the short term and some longer, but at least those precious moments of fame is what makes each of us memorable.

I remember Mrs. McNally who always left several slices of bacon on a plate on Sunday morning when the family went to church. I would enter the McNally home and sit pleasurably at the kitchen table munching on the crisp cold bacon. I was perhaps four or five years old. My parents kept the kosher food laws and no pork ever entered our house. Mrs. McNally must have observed how eagerly I had eaten bacon at some time in her home and from then on there was a silent conspiracy between us.

Every Sunday, the plate of bacon was waiting for me and I was alone to relish the taste and silently eat. I don't remember if I thanked her, but "Thank you, Mrs. McNally, even if it's a little late in the day and I don't know if you're alive. You were one of my first heroes. Your fame was your kindness and discretion."

There was the time when I was just starting school, Minnie Cloe's father often drove us to school in a big car with running boards and high seats. He would let me ride on the running board. Small children were considered too unruly to ride in such a precarious manner, but he quietly allowed me the pleasure of standing and holding on firmly with the wind whipping my hair while I rejoiced in riding so adventurously to school.

Thank you, Minnie Cloe's father. You understood a child's need to feel free and you gave me the choice and the privilege to be a cowboy on the running boards of your car.

Years later, Mrs. Brock, whose husband worked on the railroad. They lived across the street in what was called a railroad house; one room led directly back to another room directly back to the kitchen. Mrs. Brock couldn't care less about keeping house and it showed. The rooms contained beds and large tin cans.

This woman was a champion snuff-spitter. The love of her life was her flower garden. She had a garden filled with flowers of every variety and she spent every day and almost every hour tending her garden. She was always surrounded by a glorious array of flowers and scents. In the middle of this unstructured garden was a large goldfish pond. My cat spent many hours on the edging waiting to scoop up a goldfish. She might have caught a few, I really don't know. Mrs. Brock spent a lot of time chasing her away from the pond. One day, my cat came home soaking wet. Obviously she had gotten over-ambitious and fell in the pond. I think that discouraged her. I seem to remember Mrs. Brock no longer yelled "Go home cat!" anymore.

The Brock family made ice cream from fresh cow's milk (they had a cow) in an ice cream churn which seemed to take forever to produce ice cream. Everybody took turns with the handle. It went on for hours and then the result. I didn't think is was as good as drug store ice cream, but the pleasure of the family taking part (even the cow) made it very special.

Mrs. Brock gave me a white rose to pin to my dress on my first date. And I remember her smile. Thank you, Mrs. Brock.

I'M NOT HERE

June 12, 1993

I'm going through the motions,
but I'm not here.
I don't show much emotion;
I'm not here.
My mouth is talking;
I'm not here.
I hear the squawking;
I'm not here.
I fix a meal;
I'm not here.
It's so unreal;
I'm not here!
If I was here, where would I be?
In all the same places,
seeing all the same faces.
If I was here, would I be me?
The me that was me
has no definition.
I sometimes feel
I'm an apparition.
So I write and scribble;
It seems like so much drivel.
Through this haze
I'll find my way out
of this maze.
Meanwhile, I'm drifting
through the past I am sifting,
Capturing kernels of memories,
leaves of smiles.
Where did it all go?
I've traveled thousands of miles;
I don't question life.
I don't question death.
You walk; run through life
till you give out of breath!

HAPPY BIRTHDAY

June 16, 1993

I said as I was wished "Happy Birthday" this morning, "What else is new?"

I'm not for sure, new that is. I have lived these many years and perhaps in some ways I'm wiser, but the more I live the more I know that I don't know. Mostly, it doesn't bother me. It seems as if I've always given myself a wide margin for error, thereby enabling me to give other people enough room to be wrong, inaccurate and sometimes not as compassionate as I wish they could be. But then I move off into the breeze and let the winds of time blow me in whatever direction or destination will be my lot for the day or days.

I hate long-term plans. I hate to feel that I must and yet again I hate to feel there are no plans at all. I don't trust fate implicitly. I realize one's destiny relies on self and even as I let myself be blown here and there, I know I can stop whenever I tire of the flotsam and jetsam of life. I know I am focused and I know I am centered. I just don't have a single object or person to focus or center on.

So many years my life was simple. I knew what to do and when to do it and who to do it for or do it with. The selfishness of aloneness is something new to me. Freedom unfocused is freedom, but it is like a kite or balloon sailing through the air with no one holding the end of the string. No strings attached gives me a feeling of unease.

Finian, my cat, is the only string attached. He gives me cozy comfort for brief moments in the evening by curling up in my lap. He sleeps near me at night, keeping me awake much of the time with his grooming and searching for fleas. He wakes me early to be fed or to be let out into his world. Without Finian, I might just drift off into space never to be seen again. We eat, we sleep, we go back and forth.

If there is anyone looking down on us, we must look like very small disorganized armies of ants going everywhere and nowhere. I remember the joke about the man who was searching for the meaning of life. After much money and effort, he finally confronted this holy man on top of a mountain in Tibet and asked him the question: "What is the meaning of life?"

The holy man replied, "Life is an umbrella."

The man became furious and said, "After all these miles and money spent to find you, all you tell me is 'Life is an umbrella'?!"

The holy man looked very disturbed and asked, "Life isn't an umbrella?"

I understand completely. Life is an umbrella or whatever you think life is or what it means to you. Life is short and no one definition is possible. We all come to the end of our days asking in one form or another, "Is life an umbrella?"

OVER MY SHOULDER

June 17, 1993

We all have flashbacks, but today while reading something in the paper about small children and their cleverness, I was back running into the small grocery store several blocks from where I was born and lived until age seven. A sour-faced store keeper we continuously harassed by our small bodies and small devious minds.

Every time you opened or closed the screen door, a bell would tinkle and then again upon leaving the same bell would sound. We did buy candy there when we had money and it would take us an interminable amount of time to choose. He would look annoyed and say several times, "Have you made up your mind?"

Eventually, of course, we would, but what was a precursor of my life to come, I was a very discerning shopper. It had to look good and it had to taste good and of course, was I able to afford it? Little did I know that the child that was me would become the adult that is me. On one level, I am discerning with apparent good taste and good common sense.

When we left the store after our thoughtful purchase, I could never resist to run back and swing open the door, the bell ringing and run away with the door slamming and the bell madly jingling! Looking back down the street from a safe distance, the proprietor was at the front of his store, yelling words of indignation at my small figure disappearing from view.

This small child, too, has followed me into my adult life. I have a comedic view of authority and the more authoritarian a person, or persons, become, the more necessary it is for me to *tweak their noses,* to laugh at their superior/inferior demeanor and open a door (figuratively) and run away in amusement. I mean no malice. It just seems no one should take themselves so seriously.

A little patience, a little humor and the ability to let each of us be or do whatever we are involved with at the moment goes a long way to feeling good. Feeling good is not a simplistic phrase. It is a very, very important phrase which shouldn't be reduced to an inane expression.

The child that was me is the impetuous adult that is me. The child that loved cats is the adult that loved cats. This could go on endlessly, but I suppose the lesson I am learning is to look back at the child and see how she felt or mostly acted to whatever corner she turned.

I like the child that was me; I like the adult that is me. Now that I have patted myself on the back I can return to the actualization of my life. I will look back from time to time and see how that laughing child took each day in her stride and how she grew up to be me.

TO DARIA
(THANK YOU, OGDEN NASH)

June 17, 1993

What is this thing called rejection,
upon very close inspection?
It must be a figment of your imagination;
or maybe plain frustration.
Rejection is a state of seeing.
So, upon profound reflection
I don't see any rejection.

II
(THANK YOU, EDGAR ALLAN POE)

Once upon a daytime heated
while I pondered and retreated,
upon many things and many places long ago
suddenly there came a sound.
I thought perhaps I'd become unwound.
But it was only the window shades swinging back and fro.

BIRDS BEGIN TO SING

June 18, 1993

Four and twenty blackbirds baked into a pie;

When the pie was opened, the birds began to sing.
Isn't that a funny dish to sit before a king?

The blackbirds are beginning to sing.
I haven't heard music for a long time.

The king was in the counting house,
counting out his money.
The queen was in the parlor
eating bread and honey.
The maid was in the garden
hanging out the clothes.
Along came a blackbird
and bit off her nose.

It seems the theme for today is blackbirds. They are a lively bunch though not terribly sociable. I am sociable and not terribly black, but we do have something in common.

I love the freedom of flight the birds pursue and I love the singing of birds. I can hear the humming in my heart and the beginning of a melody. The melodic sounds of life which I heard in the distance are now coming closer and are now beginning to envelop me in their soothing embrace.

Life is truly remarkable. Even after sorrow, living is still so full of music. It just takes time, patience and the ability to listen to the songs. I can well visualize four and twenty blackbirds singing in a pie; what a joyous choir, singing something in the language of birds!

We were put into a pie
and didn't die.
And when the pie was opened,
and we began to sing.
We realized we were alive.
Intact, each with our wings.

FATHER'S DAY

June 20, 1993

My father died in November 1952. He was sixty-seven years old. I wasn't living in San Francisco when he died, but I had visited twice during the last year of his life; once when he had become ill and again later in the year. It was inevitable. Death from a cancer that had invaded the liver was insidious and there was no stopping death.

We had grown to be friends. I never knew my father. He had been raised in Europe and it had followed him to the United States. Children were always kept in a different category. I tried to cross the line many times, but seldom did, I find a happy friend on the other side. Occasionally, he would tell me a little about his youth, but I never shared my dreams with him, knowing instinctively that it would either embarrass him or anger him. He was my father, and in retrospect I find myself telling people about his intellectual pursuits, his organized persona and his unfulfilled dreams of coming to a strange country and remaining a stranger till the day he died.

I remember the day he died. I was back in another state. He requested to be returned to the state in which I resided then, and to the city in which I was born, to be buried next to his son, my brother, who died too soon and much too young.

I had loved my brother who was older than me. My brother was my parent, acting with all the reason and compassion of an adult. He was a child of our country and knew the ways of our world. My father, on the other hand, had never adapted and though he tried, he was always a misfit in this country and I, the child, sensed this alienation and had turned to my brother for guidance.

After my brother died, I don't remember much about my father except his weekly long walks out to the cemetery to visit my brother's grave. Every Sunday around noon, he would announce "I'm going to the cemetery."

It was several miles and the summer heat was unforgiving. I was always angry at him for going and especially announcing his going. I knew my mother must have felt a sharp stab of pain at the mention for my brother. I felt he was needlessly rubbing salt in her wounds.

My mother and brother were much closer than father and son. My mother mourned my brother all her life, but never verbalized her pain. I asked her many years later why I never saw her cry when I was a child. She said she couldn't afford to cry because it would have made me sad and it was very important to her that I not be reminded of this terrible tragedy in our lives. My mother many years later when she was quite old and we made out our respective wills, insisted my brother's name be mentioned. "Yes," she said. "I have two children."

Looking back on my father's weekly sojourn to the cemetery which lasted until we left the state, I think it was some kind of penance. This son whom he couldn't relate to in life had to be acknowledged in death. It was my father wearing his own "Sackcloth and ashes."

My father, my intelligent, sensitive, handsome father. My father, my timid, introverted unhappy father. I loved you. You are a part of me. The part of me that knows you respects you and the other part of me is in my genes and the hand that is writing this. We shared unspoken words, but I am sharing them with you now. I am your daughter.

After you died, one of your sisters visited my mother and said you had written her many letters and talked about me. She said that you called me the "sunshine in your life." You gave me life and I gave you the warmth of the sun. Now that my sun is setting I will always remember I was your "sunshine."

THE MAGICIAN

June 21, 1993

Talking on the phone, or otherwise, and moving out and about, I know who I am. I am me and I'm alive! When I'm alone and the sounds of other voices subsides, I disappear. This disappearing act has been going on for months, but I couldn't put a name to it.

Now out of my bag of tricks, I have identified the one that is most disturbing. I'm a good juggler. I can juggle schedules, lunches and shopping. I can use one hand or the other to catch the moving objects in my time and space. My magic tricks are simple and complex. I can make different people appear at different times. They are interesting, at least to me, and a kaleidoscope of cultures, dreams and ambitions; beautiful patterns of people superimposed on my life. I can do a tightrope walk, wavering but never falling off. It seems I've practiced this for years and it's one of my easier tricks.

But the disappearing act is a hard one to handle. I have that strange feeling in the pit of my stomach and a tightening in my face that makes me wary and concerned. What if I disappear and don't come back? What if one of these days I will be gone forever? I know that it's inevitable, but not now and not in the middle of my life or at least the last quarter.

I feel like I am slipping away and holding on to pull myself back to reality. I think I am going to try and eliminate this part of my repertoire. After all, the famous magician Houdini went too far and his magic finished him off. We take our skills for granted, but there comes a time for deletion and possible addition. This disappearing act, which was probably hovering about, intruded itself into my act. I will have to wave my magic wand and eliminate it. *Be gone, be gone!*

I now will have to get back to the drawing board and create a more user-friendly imaginative and wondrous trick. "The trick is that there is no trick, only reality in many forms and laughter in many dark corners."

TALKING ALOUD

June 23, 1993

I've been reading today's paper and I just told you that someone well-known died. Then I realized that you, too, were dead, but I had to tell you out loud the tidbits of news which, I shared with you for so many years. I think I will have to keep talking to you, asking your advice or opinions. I don't know if there is another world or not after death, but since I knew you so well and your reactions, I can hear your words in my mind.

I know how you felt about most things and how sometimes you became exasperated, but mostly I can hear you saying "You make the decision, you know I'll go along with it."

And so I made a decision. I am consumed by indecision now, but if I sit quietly or walk through the house and talk to you, the answer seems to come drifting into my senses and I act upon it. You might not be here in person, but I feel so very deeply that I still need to tell you things, even nonsensical things.

I need to see your face set in your serious thinking mode, your pleasurable appreciative mode and your warm smile. I somehow feel that you need to hear my voice, since you no longer have eyes to see, you can still hear and I have no problem talking into empty space knowing that wherever you are, you are listening and sharing my life. Just because you're gone from this earth doesn't mean you're not somewhere and I have to keep communicating with this internal feeling that I so strongly have that you can hear me.

I've been doing many frivolous things and spent moneys, not too much, but more than I should, on clothes. I'm not only starting a new life, I'm starting a new wardrobe. You are shaking your head and saying, "Do you really need all that stuff?, and I'm saying, "Not really, but enjoying the childish abandon I have been experiencing by being impractical."

Then your voice says to me, "You know I've never really stopped you from buying." And I know that is true and I know I have to settle down to something more fulfilling than eating lunches and buying clothes. I need to make you proud of me. I will try. There is no one else I would like to please more than you, living or dead.

DREAMS

June 24, 1993

I dream nightly, but most often push the dreams back into the darkness when I awaken. There is a storehouse of dreams in some dark corner of my mind and there they shall remain, but last night's dream is here walking with me in the daylight. Is it symbolic? I don't know.

I dreamt that I was in a city on a beach and gazing at a barrier reef in the distance. It looked so inviting. Trees and flowers and small buildings. It wasn't very far and I put my feet into the water and the water was warm, but I can't swim. I thought perhaps I could make it as I didn't think it was very far. Some kind person, I think it was a woman, said ,"Don't worry, I'll fix it." And proceeded to build a small dam across the water and I walked swiftly on the wet sand that narrowly marked my way to the island.

I entered a small cafe in the shape of a ship, probably like a fishing boat. People were seated at tables and eating. I became hungry and went to a window and asked what the cutlet being served was. They told me it was "fried worms." I was repelled! Fried worms; it doesn't look like worms.

They proceeded to show me long grayish worms and said they are fried, they flatten out, but it is still worms. The ship (cafe) began rocking, rocking wildly and overturned and I was thrown in the water. It was only a short distance from the shore so I was soon on the land, safe and unharmed.

I looked across and the ship (cafe) was lying on its side. I asked what is going to happen. Everyone shrugged their shoulders unknowingly and in an indifferent manner. While I was looking at the overturned boat, it somehow righted itself and stood proudly upright in the position it had been standing. I looked across the water in awe!

I was confused about my precarious journey, and my return from this so-called barrier reef. A dream is only a dream, but it is good to find myself awake in my own house on my own land.

WASTE

June 25, 1993

You have been gone two-hundred and seventy-eight days. Imagine two-hundred and seventy-eight days without you! How have I filled these days? I can look back over my calendar and reconstruct days, days filled with people and lunches and meetings and shopping (which I did till I'm dropping). Days, endless days. Time spent frivolously and meaninglessly. Time needed to be used up wastefully.

Once I had a purpose. You were my purpose and now I have the endless days at my disposal. Lovely, beautiful days; sunny, foggy spaces in time and I drift through them, walk through them, run through them. I would like to store them in a safe place and preserve them for the time if that time ever comes to use these very precious days for something satisfying.

Tomorrow is almost here: day two-hundred and seventy-nine and I don't know what to do with it. I feel the days slipping through my fingers. I hate waste, most of all time. Time relaxing isn't waste. Time uncharted isn't waste, but time unshared is waste. So begins another empty day.

NOW THE DAY IS OVER

June 26, 1993

When I was very young and striving to be a poet like my father, I wrote a poem that started like this:

Now the day is over,
it is getting dark.
I no more see the clover,
I no more see the lark.

Obviously I had been reading some of the poets who wrote these types of lyrical lines. I am now much, much older and I feel like writing something in a similar vein.

My life has progressed through so many changes and moves and of course, the most recent, the death of a husband of many years and my poem if I could write as I feel, would be something like this:

Now the day is over;
it is getting dark.
I look out from my window
and I see the park.
I think of days we spent
walkin' round the lake.
Oh, to have you back with me;
instead I have an ache!
I talk, I laugh, I chatter;
I'm handling it so well.
Believe me folks,
it's all a joke.
I really feel like hell!

ATTENTION MUST BE PAID

June 27,1993

Today I had lunch with fifteen people. Fifteen people, fifteen stories. Since all of us have lived for many years, our stories are long. I couldn't talk at length with anyone, more's the pity.

I did speak briefly with one woman from Germany, whose story I am sure is long and sad. All I really heard was when she came to this country in the nineteen-thirties and moved to El Paso, Texas, which is on the border of Mexico, she was anxious to learn English. Her co-workers were Mexicans so therefore Spanish is her second language. These many years later she has great difficulty with the English language.

Then my friend sitting next to me is a remarkable survivor of World War II, the blitz in London and among her many stories, I feel like I've entered the World of Charles Dickens, perhaps a century later. It's filled with the fogs of London and the Caste system and the eventual heroic ending of happiness and success in the New World, but not without the traces of bruises from the past.

There were smiling faces, gentle glances and I know behind each of them lies a story worth telling and more importantly worth listening to. I would wish I were many people. I would want to hear all their words. I would want them to know that someone cares. My heart is saddened for all the stories never told and for all the lack of concern for each and every one.

We are born, we grow up, we live our lives to the best we can. Then if we are lucky, we grow old and we die. When no one is listening or no attention is paid, I am saddened, I am truly saddened. We all deserve our moment in the sun, we all deserve some small reward for living. Life is a wonderful gift, but the price is high. The absence of some acknowledgment is the saddest thing of all.

I, too, crave attention. I, too, want someone to listen. I, too, want my days on earth to have some small meaning. Most of us will go quietly into that good night. Most of us will be forgotten when those who knew us no longer talk of us. That is as it should be, but now while we are alive, hear us! We are still living, breathing entities! Don't turn away; each of us in our own season like a leaf will fall from the tree of life and be blown away, forever. *Attention must be paid, attention!*

IN THE BEGINNING

June 28, 1993

I've been trying to makes sense of it all. I've not sat down and thought about what I've been doing. Once in a while, it crosses my mind that I've been doing a whirling-dervish kind of dance these last months. My husband died eight months ago. I was alone. I had no support group. With a minimal number of family members who were a brief presence during the time around his death and soon disappeared into their own world, never to be seen again or hardly ever.

Instinctively, I began creating my own extended family. I went out into the stores and bought clothes or food and I engaged in conversations with whomever happened to be friendly. We would talk and some of them became friends. Some, I touched with my magic wand and for a few minutes or an hour, they became my sister, my cousin or whatever role I assigned them.

Many, many people have passed through my life these past months. As I was creating and developing my own support group, I felt I was growing stronger, more resilient or sometimes even frighteningly monster-like in that I felt I could take over the world, my world, and create my own people, people whom I could give and care about and who in turn would be my family. I have started my world and if the bible is true and God created the world in seven days, I am certainly not godlike.

It's been eight months and though I am creating my world, it is far from being complete. This strength that is emanating from me is sometimes good and other times seems to be a sham. I think perhaps I've read more into my ability to create and that this world I am creating will go up in a puff of smoke. I will be alone again.

I venture forth each day and could easily add another member to my congregation. There are no dues, there are no rules for my people. They can come and go as they like. I want no one to feel chained or duty-bound. All actions must be spontaneous and given freely. This strange power that I feel now will probably dissipate in time when and if I become focused more intently on someone or something.

For the moment though, I need to feel I am important and capable and humorous. I know I am, but without anyone to reinforce my presence, I am nothing. I realize that all through my life I have been my own best friend and therein lies the clue for whatever strength I have, whatever magic I can perform, whatever brings people toward me who find in me something akin to love, love of mankind.

There have been times I have wanted to embrace the whole world. The world and its inhabitants need love and so many, too many, live lives of quiet desperation. I want to give desperation a voice. Every voice should be heard by someone, somewhere.

Maybe that's what my role is in this life; to listen, to talk, of course, but in the main, to listen. Everyone in this world has something to say and in my role as "Every man," I will try to be the universal ears.

FLASHBACKS

June 28, 1993

I've read and heard about people who have had flashbacks. Vietnam veterans suddenly being transported back to deaths in the jungle of Vietnam; horrible, searing scenes of gunfire, explosions and fear, constant fear.

Will I be next? Who will be next? Holocaust survivors, who I am sure spend their lives with sudden flashbacks of concentration camps, starvation, acrid smell of burning bodies, walls of faces, desperate faces with unseeing eyes, skeleton bodies diminished in death, though yet not buried.

I have always had great empathy for all who have suffered through wars and imprisonment, but it has been from a distance. I would classify my emotions as impersonally personal, but now my turn has come. I am now a victim of flashbacks.

I can be reading the paper in the midst of an article relating to nothing of importance and my mind is thrown back into the hospital and I look down and see that my husband's kidney failure is now complete. "There is no hope, you are truly dying."

I go downstairs and bring up some root beer for you to drink. They would not allow any food or liquid by mouth these last two weeks. "Damn it! You are going to taste something you like before you die! You sip a little of root beer. I ask you if it tastes good and you nod your head. A simple thing; a sip of root beer and you nod "yes."

My flashbacks continue through my days and through my nights. I put a picture of our cat, Finian, upon the wall of your room while you were still more aware. You were so pleased when someone admired him. A nurse said, "He looks like a Maine 'coon."

And you smiled, "Yes, that's my kid!"

You enjoyed the pancakes for breakfast once in the hospital before you entered the twilight zone of your life. I brought cassettes from home with the radio-cassette player so you could hear music you liked. I held your hand and I know you heard the music, but you drifted in and out and told me several times, "I'm dying."

I wanted you to know I was near, I wanted to believe a miracle would happen. You were not dying. I never said the word. I never thought the word. You would not die, you could not die!

I spent the last day stroking your arms. I sat by your bed; you were still so handsome. I see you every day, I see you alive and well and I see you dying. My flashbacks are constant and come and go throughout the day. There is absolutely nothing in my life that doesn't bring you back into my consciousness. Perhaps someday down the road these flashbacks will be fewer and less vivid. I think I will miss them, as tragic as they are. As long as I still see you and feel you so intensely, you are not dead. You are breathing in my mind. You're telling me all the things I've heard again and again in my brain.

Flashbacks; the word doesn't begin to describe what I feel, but I guess one name is just as good as another. It's up to us, the survivors, to call it as we feel it and describe what our internal view of our emotions reveal to us.

We are a character in our own play and as our memories change, so do the scenes. I think your last words to me were, "Stay, stay!" I will hear these words until the day I die.

You are not dead! No, I am not in denial! You are too much a part of me to be dead. I can quote you. I can share your views as I can share our home. You are not dead! You have just gone away. I know you won't return, but I know I will be joining you someday and then we will be dead together!

FLYING SOLO

June 29, 1993

I've never given it a name, but now I think *flying solo* is just about as close as I can get to trying to figure out what I am doing now. Flying solo has many facets. One part of it is fear. Broad, deep fear. Fear that there will be no one to take over if the flying gets rough or you're just not up to whatever it is that you are doing.

Fear. That is the biggest obstacle to flying solo. The first thing to getting started is pushing yourself off into space. You're hesitant, you're reluctant, but eventually you go for it. You move out. You're flying a little precariously with no direction and no destination, but you're flying. You have to keep getting up, getting out and some days you "stay in bed," so to speak and wait for that internal energy to return and recharge your battery. Soon you're up and off again.

Flying solo has many downsides, but it also has many ups. For instance, being alone gives you an opportunity to see the view from your own eyes, no other, good or bad it's your scene. There is always an underlying sadness of beauty unshared, but since you are no longer accountable to anyone, you can do your share of uncontrolled flips and flops and experience new and interesting vistas which you could never have encountered with a co-pilot.

You are in control of your own destiny. It is exhilarating at times and much of the time you have a feeling of uneasiness. It's not fear, it's not panic, it's the aloneness of decision-making; the aloneness of no one to either reprimand you or stroke you. There are many times I am stranded in my own dizziness, but determined to make the flight, I hang in there and complete each day's journey.

Flying solo; many people never experience it and many would not want to take the trip. Not everyone can pass the test, but I feel that there's enough of me that's in working order and what a shame it would be to put myself in storage for the duration. Soon I will take off again and each day come in for a safe landing at my own home base. What a feeling! In the wide blue yonder, flying solo!

THE UNMENTIONABLE

11:27 P.M., July 2, 1993

I went to bed and as I reached over to touch your pillow, I thought during all our years of marriage and all our hours of conversation, we never ever talked about the unmentionable. We never talked about death, our deaths, what we would do if the other one died, how we would handle it, what we hoped the other would do.

We never ever talked about the unmentionable. We've all read and heard about the untouchables in India. A caste of people despised and denied recognition by the rest of country. For some reason, I seem to find a similarity between these sad discarded untouchables and the subject which was unmentionable through all our years of living and sharing every facet of our lives.

I know what I would have told you if per chance I had died first. I think this is what I would have said. First, I would have said, "Thank you for all our years together, thank you for being my friend and for standing by me all through my life. Thank you for caring and supporting me during illness and uncertainty. I know you will grieve, you will cry, you will feel lost and alone. I would never have left you willingly. These are choices in which we have no part. Mourn for awhile, but not too long. I don't want to go out of this world leaving you sad. I want to think that I gave you enough happiness that you will soon find laughter and joy in the rest of your life. I want you to wake in the morning and relish the beauty of the world I no longer inhabit. I want you to feel the warmth of the sun and remember the warmth of my hand in yours and smile. I want you to feel a deep peace because you gave me happiness, you gave me love. I want you to be happy because you deserve to live a full life even if I am not with you."

"The unmentionable is now a reality. It is death and since it is inevitable, I would hope you come to terms with it. It is a part of the life cycle. We are born, we live and we die. Not everyone is as lucky as we were to have shared our lives with someone special, someone who knew what each other was thinking, someone who put each other first in all the ways of our life."

"The unmentionable, the ending of life, is the more tragic if one hasn't experienced the fullness and joy of companionship and total trust and love with another human being."

"I will miss you forever, but I would hope my legacy to you would be to "remember me," but please don't cry too long, don't mourn too long. You still have much to give and much to share. It will not be the same, but don't waste the rest of your life in grieving. Life is for the living and whoever has the gift of life should use it well. It is much too precious to waste a single drop."

"The sad untouchables of India are outcasts in their world. Do not let the unmentionable make you an outcast in your world and cause you to deny yourself happiness."

ALMOST INDEPENDENCE DAY

July 3, 1993

Today is July 3, 1993. I thought it was July the Fourth. Tomorrow I will be watching the fireworks in the distance.

You and I have been watching them for many years. We could hear the boom and then the beautiful flares of many colors in bursts of round shapes, stars and all the colors of the universe. The night sky will be a spectacle of happy colors! It has always make me feel so joyful! The child within loves the sound and fury of fireworks.

It seems to be a reinforcement of living and a happy colorful display of enchantment. Tomorrow I won't be able to share this with you. I will turn silently and say, "Look at that! Just look at that!"

And you will say, "That was a big one!"

I dreamt of you again last night. You came home and I gave you your electric shaver and said, "I'm glad I didn't give this away, but I did give away most of your clothes."

You said, "That's okay. I can always buy more clothes." But you seem pleased that I had kept your razor. I told you I was expecting a friend and that she thought you were dead. You said, "That's all right, she'll see me and it won't matter."

"I was very apprehensive, but very pleased, so very pleased that you weren't dead. You looked wonderful! You looked rested like you had been on a leisurely vacation. I wondered why I had thought you were dead. This dream was short-lived and I woke alone and knew you were gone."

"Why are my dreams teasing me? Why do I dream you are with me and then I awake to reality. *Now you see it; now you don't!* You are embedded so deep in my psyche that I will dream of you off and on the rest of my life. At least in my dreams you are happy, content and well!"

"You are not the man who lay dying in the hospital last fall. He is gone. He lay dying for three long weeks and he died from an illness with no name. He died from liver failure due to Hepatitis C, which he contacted in the hospital. He went in to repair his hip and left with a mystery death."

I have been assuring myself with the words, "It was his time," but I don't believe that for a second! It was not his time. He went in joyful that he would come out the better for it (the operation). The operation was a success and he would have been the better for it.

"No! It was not his time! Through negligence, indifference, or error, he was transfused with poisonous blood and he was a victim. Now I am the victim and I don't know if I can do anything about it. I don't want revenge, but it would be gratifying to right a wrong. Nothing will bring him back except in my dreams, but someone somewhere should accept the responsibility for a wrongful death. I will pursue this course even if it is a dead end."

My cat has just come in to offer me solace or company or just to come in. He has strolled out on the deck and has ensconced himself on the chaise lounge. He seems to appear when I begin going down into sadness and he brightens my day by rolling in the sun on the deck and giving me meows of conversation. We talk and then he repairs to his lounge to groom and stretch in the sun.

Tomorrow is July the Fourth. My first Independence Day without you. I will watch the fireworks and still find pleasure in the bright colors, but they will never look the same without you by my side. I still say that "it was not your time." I have not said these words to anyone,; on the contrary, I say "I guess it was his time. It seems the simplest thing to say and it seems to comfort anyone who has gone through a death. I really don't know anything about death, except that life as we know it, is over. When my time comes, perhaps someone, somewhere will say, "It was her time."

WHAT DO I DO?

July 4, 1993

What do I do with my days?
Where have they all gone?
I know I slept and then I wake;
and then again it's dawn.

What do I do with my days?
How do they pass from sight?
I'm not doing anything
and lo and behold, it's night.

What do I do with my days?
I look out; the sun is shining.
I've been nibbling my time away.
It does keep me from pining.

What do I do with my days?
I know, I throw away hours
on frivolous tasks and meanderings
instead of savoring the flowers!

What do I do with my days?
My nights are filled with the dark.
I should be involved in something special,
something that has a spark!

What do I do with my days?
I feel them slipping by.
I am awake to nothing,
waiting for me to die.

Don't know what I do with my days.
Haven't got a clue.
I only know I have to go on.
I'll always be missing you!

INVASION AVERTED

July 7, 1993

The walls are beginning to close in on me and there is no one to push them back. Maybe my pen will block their movement. Maybe the written word will become my shield and protect me from the invasion of the hordes of sad emotions that are surrounding me.

I thought I had everything pretty much in control, but obviously I was deluding myself. Delusion is a friendly ally, but since it can be blown away so easily by reality, it can not be relied upon to be a long-term friend. Delusion, illusion, all lovely creatures that we all reside with, but when push comes to shove, they evaporate.

Reality, on the other hand, is always nearby; sometimes only glimpsed at brief moments and sometimes coming face to face with you. Today, reality has moved into my presence. It is sitting here with me, walking with me, driving with me. I would wish it away, but today it is persistent. I felt a few days ago that it wasn't going to let me play games with it much longer; it has been patient, but I've lived closely with reality all my life and even though it has kept its own council and sat quietly by, it knew I had accepted it and acknowledged it.

For the past months, it has let me wander afar into another realm that has been soothing, busy, but devoid of any real meaning. I guess I will just have to face reality in the face now or very soon. It doesn't seem to want to hover in the distance anymore.

I was doing so well, wasn't I? I was moving along so well, wasn't I? Then why today am I experiencing dizziness and a gnawing pain in my chest and why is my vision more blurred and why and why? I have to come to terms with my grief. I have to let him go. I have allowed the dying to die, but now I have to let myself, the living, live.

I think this is the most difficult thing in the world for me to do. I'm still breathing and moving through time, but living—no! I would not call this living, just being. Living should give me joy, being is just that—being. I am full of nothing; I am empty.

Death has removed my core. The world around me sees the exterior, but no one is privy to the interior. I am glad, because I feel there is a total absence there. I thought I was building an inner self, but that was a part of the delusion. My smiling face, my joyful voice all concealed the pain, the deep, deep pain that has corroded my insides. I don't want pity. Pity has no place in my life whether expressed from others or the self-pity so many indulge in.

No! I need to start excavating my shell and start rebuilding. I have no idea what kind of structure will be created or if anything can be created at all, but my good friend "Reality," will help me decide and place a gentle hand on my back and push me toward whatever goal is out there.

The walls that are surrounding me are still standing tall and threatening, but they have stopped moving. I can breath a little easier now. I was almost suffocating from their impending march toward me! Reality gave me a sly smile and said quietly, "You can handle your new life, you really can! Just relax and don't expect too much, too soon."

RETROSPECT

July 8, 1993

In retrospect, I am looking back over the last months. I seem to have ambled out into the great big world and talked to everyone within range. I was obviously searching for myself. I was lost, I was totally lost, but I did not actively know I was lost! I just had to keep looking, relating and trying to find some connection and if I was lucky, I would find myself.

The world was a huge, gray plain. I spent small moments with the inhabitants I encountered. New inhabitants would appear and these, too, gave me small comfort for small moments. Now that my friend, Reality, has loomed large beside me, I feel that all these months and all these people were only temporary respites or pit stops on my journey. I've lived much too long to be dependent on short-term friendships with people who have lived or will live their own lives.

My life is filled with many, many memories to be no longer shared or even related to unhearing ears. I would like to share, but I am not naive enough to think that people want to listen, let alone hear. My words, my thoughts are thrown away and discarded. I am much too proud to continue to be wasteful with myself. I have much more worth and I must continue to reinforce my worth by keeping my own counsel.

It has been a learning experience for me. I want to give and want to listen. I did both. Except in rare cases, I came out the loser. I find I am enervated and yet, very few have truly given me solace. Perhaps no one can. Perhaps I need something no one is prepared to give or has the ability to give. It seems to me a basic garden variety friendship is all I can expect, but most people are greedy and only want to take.

I can plant, water and nurture other gardens, but no one wants to climb beyond their own fence. It would behoove me to plant, water and nurture my own garden. It's a lonely job, but somebody's got to do it!

THEY'VE ALL GONE

July 8, 1993

They've all gone. We said our good-byes. Who will say good-bye to me? They've all gone, the good, the bad, the beautiful, the not so beautiful. They were here, they were so very here and now they are gone. We say good-bye to someone most days, a casual good-bye and then the final good-bye!

So much has gone, so many fine minds, so many gracious people, so many, oh, so many. I mourn them all! I mourn for all the last good-byes over the centuries. I mourn for the husbands, wives, mothers, fathers, sons, daughters. I mourn for all those who went before me.

My life at times is consumed with mourning and I wonder where it all went. Where did the centuries go? Are they perhaps hidden some place in the universe? Was it all a magician's trick? Were we ever here and if we were, where did we disappear to? Life is a puzzle within a puzzle. I know I'll never put all the pieces together, but my mind is constantly scrambling about to find an answer or at least an accommodation with whatever space I am occupying at this time in history.

I know this sounds very metaphysical. So be it. We are all searchers one way or another.

BUSY, BUSY!

July 9, 1993

It has been so many months since you died. Many months, not many years. Your death keeps nibbling at me like a mouse at the cheese. I keep putting it behind me, to the side of me. I file it under D for death, S for sorrow, G for grief, and sometimes even T for terror.

As soon as I have quiet time when I have finished doing my mundane chores and settle down to read or some other innocuous pastime, you join me. I welcome you, but you're not here, only my memories are here and I sometimes feel you're watching me. It is an eerie feeling and when I start writing, it seems you vanish or at least the overwhelming sadness surrounding me is diminished.

I am truly diminished. There will never be anyone I can turn to in the same way. I know it is not realistic to expect life to go on forever, but I don't want to be realistic. I want things to be the way they were before you died. I am dying, too. We all are, but now I feel my dying has accelerated and is running along beside me, not every day, but it is always waiting to jog beside me.

Keep busy, keep busy! The code words for the survivors, but how busy can you keep? I am tired to death of *keeping busy*! I shake my head and think, "..so what are you going to do?" What can you do? Tomorrow is another day and soon night will come and if I am lucky, I will sleep and I will wake to another day! There is absolutely no one in the world that I can connect with. Whatever intellect I have is floating around in limbo. The only true friend I have now are my words, my written words.

I keep wondering how you would appraise my written words. I have come about again from anger at your death, denial of your death, guilt passed me by and I don't know the other labels attached to the stages that we widows and widowers are supposed to encounter. But I am back to anger. My anger has taken on another characteristic though. I am angry at your death, but now my anger is directed at some of the living.

Perhaps this is healthy. Perhaps my anger will give me the strength of my convictions. I have convictions, I have opinions and I have let them drift aimlessly and have been tossed like flotsam and jetsam in the stream of the days of my life. No more, no more! My anger now will become productive. I will start to take charge of my life, my ego, myself.

I always thought I did take charge, but now I realize that was a fallacy. You were in charge and that was good. You were wise , you were compassionate and I had a free ride on your coattails! What a time for me to become an independent woman at this time in my life! Mostly I have a handle on the usual problems, but I find I have an *Achilles heel,* which is my inability to say "No" on a social level. I have begun to say no, but there is a price to pay. Of course there's always a price to pay!

I have to accept loneliness, I have to accept indifference and of course, rejection. I have to strengthen my inner core and learn to live the single life! I was a good student once. Perhaps this new learning experience will not be too difficult if I don't fight and relax and breathe in the newness.

I have always marched to the sound of a different drummer. Maybe at this time of my life I will be more alert to the sounds since this is the first time I am hearing them with my ears only. Maybe I will be marching in unison with my own intuition, my own sensitivity, my own person! Then maybe, your death will take its place in a loving memory and I can truly let you rest in peace!

MY SOUL TO TAKE

12:16 A.M., July 10, 1993

Now I lay me down to sleep,
I pray the Lord my soul to keep.
If I should die before I wake,
I pray the Lord my soul to take.

A child's prayer. I said this as a child and it was comforting. I am a child no longer and when I lay me down to sleep, I only hope for sleep. And when I pray, if I should pray, I would not pray for my soul. I don't know what a soul consists of and if it does exist, I would pray for many souls. If I should die, and I will die, it would be good to not waken to pain. The last, the last line, "my soul to take" seems a limited departure. I would expect not only my soul, but all the rest of me to accompany my soul. Perhaps my essence, my spirit or whatever it was that made me—me.

I probably should not dissect a child's prayer; sweet words of comfort, but the cynic within me begins asking questions in the wee hours of the night. I know there are no answers, only questions. Ma nishta? Why, why?

ANOTHER SKIRMISH

July 10, 1993

My old pain is revisiting me. My old friend, I use the word loosely. When you've made friends with pain, the pain, though still not one of your favorites, at least for whatever time it inhabits your body, seems to be a part-time friend. This friend, unfortunately, has lived with me too often and for too long. Since I don't have much choice in the matter I make it, him, her, or whatever as comfortable as possible.

All through our lives some of us will have pain; some more, some less. I don't know where I am on the scale of pain, but I know it well. Give it a comfortable place to sit, give it a warm bed to sleep in, give it whatever nourishment is necessary to satisfy its hunger and thirst. Then close your eyes and hope it won't stay too long.

Reconcile yourself to this unruly friend and sooner or later you will contain it, tame it, and then it will silently slip away. You know it will be back, but never anticipate its arrival. Once it's back in your doorstep, the routine becomes second nature. You learn to endure. Never, ever fight this foe. Let it run its course and leave of its own free will. At least you are not the conqueror, but more importantly, you are not the conquered.

I am full of words. I am up to the top and overflowing! I am a flood that is consuming not only the forks of the river and beyond. I am the wind that not only blows heartily and strong, but a tornado, a cyclone that whisks up everything in its path. I am the rain, the drenching downpour and the storm and the thunder along with the lightning.

These are the words that are within me, bursting to be written. What they will say, even I don't know. I just know I am full of words. I have been sitting on a nest of words and they are ready to hatch. What they will look like is impossible to imagine! They could be underdeveloped thoughts, stumbling ideas or retarded dreams, but these words are my children and I will love them!

SHARING

July 11, 1993

Life unshared is life half-lived. Life unshared is having vision in one eye, having one hand or one foot. Mostly, mostly, pain that is shared is diluted and eased and reduced to a distant annoying sound. Joy shared is happiness plus one, or two, and happiness shared is enhanced! Colors are brighter, food is more flavorful, everything takes on an aura of pleasure!

The death of the one you shared with leaves this tremendous void and for long, long hours, days, months and maybe years, you are left dangling by your one hand and seeing with your one eye. Eventually, or so it seems to me, I am not acquiring the other eye or the other hand, but my memories of sharing give my one eye the ability to see more and my one hand to hold on tighter. And so I grow stronger!

I'll never be as complete as I was when I shared. Your strength and what you were have enabled me to live at half-mast. I can still go far at half-speed, so I am living at this reduced rate, but I still see the view and I feel the sun!

POEM

July 12, 1993

Swirling, whirling chaos
creatures of the earth!
Hearing, fearing
jagged endings,
lives unbending,
to death from careless birth.
Unceasing noise,
all willed with poise;
all wanting, not receiving.
Are still not formed
only informed
internally, not deceiving.

Swirling, whirling,
our lives we're hurling!
What is your rush to die?
Come down and rest.
You'll find what's best.
Years pass quickly by.

SISTERS OF THE 'HOOD

July 14, 1993

Widowhood. The end of a long-running show. The show is over! I have met myself and many members of this group. We've all gone through the initiation rites and we have all become full-fledged members. I think of myself as fortunate to have had such a long run! It took time to refine some of the acts and to be able to express some of the lines in a meaningful fashion.

I'm studying the last act, but I look back wistfully to the original. All in all, I think it was a splendid production! Other members of our 'hood have different story lines. Some more tragic, more humorous, more dramatic, but all in all, we are left with this emptiness that mostly for all is impossible to fathom.

I've talked and listened to others' stories. Our roles have similarities, but mostly were very different. Now we are huddled together psychologically trying to define ourselves and to play the final part in our life. We all want to do it with dignity and grace.

I need to add large portions of humor. I've always found life a bit ludicrous. I've often smiled in the face of the unknown. Perhaps it is my defense mechanism. Others have to go on and do it their way. We sisters of the 'hood have a few common denominators. We are women. We are widows. After that it is up to each of us to gather and give nourishment to each other, each in her own way, in her own time, as much or as little as each of us in capable of giving or receiving. I have received much and given as much as possible. I am preparing for the next production. In my case, I think I need to "leave them laughing"!

LEAVING CHEYENNE

July 15, 1993

The veil is lifting. The curtain is rising. I could use similes to describe what I am feeling, but most of them seem too pat, too simplistic and never really hit the nail on the head. My view is still hazy, very blurred, but now and then I see the future—my future.

I feel the sun and then revel in night lights, but it is a surface, a removed sense of awareness. I am leaving Cheyenne, which in my own terminology, is leaving a place I called home for many years. I am moving out into the future. I feel sad, lonely, alienated. I am all of these, but I am also happy, fulfilled to some extent and befriended. I must follow the rainbow, my rainbow. I must continue to revel in all the colors around me and experience the joy, even limited joy, in whatever measure passes me by.

My eyes are still clouded by my sorrow. Tears do not run down my cheeks. My tears are reserved. Maybe, they are all huddled in a corner of my soul and will remain there the rest of my life, but I know they are within me. Too many tears have been shed for too many reasons. Tears can be an outlet for sadness, joy or just for show.

I need to keep my tears for my eyes only. I need to share some of the rest of my life, but the intense emotions of my life are in my own private realm.

People often store their most precious jewels in safety deposit boxes and my most precious jewels are the love I received and the assorted memories. I open my vault on occasion and sort through the contents. Since life has an urgency about it, I must go out and about, but when I think of the rainbow, tears come to my eyes and my heart is still breaking! How do you live with a broken heart?

COMING TO TERMS

July 16, 1993

How do I love thee; let me count the ways.

It has been nine months today since you died. Nine months bring forth new life, in the form of another human being. What have these nine months brought forth for me? Let me count:

1. I can count my home and the security which has enabled me to be free of worry.
2. I can count my companion, our cat Finian, with whom we shared many pleasurable moments in his antics.
3. I can count my ability to handle the practical things in life you taught me well. I can go from getting the car fixed to having the house painted without indecision.
4. I can count the self-confidence you bestowed upon me these many years and feel at most times an inner peace.
5. I can count the compliments you bestowed on me and even though I've entered the older years still feel pretty and admired.
6. I can count the memories I have of you and so many years of being my very best friend!
7. I can count on your complete trust in me, thereby enabling me to trust my own judgment.
8. I can count on the freedom you gave me to be myself and being free to open myself to others.

I can keep on counting. New images will be emerging all the rest of my life. Most of all I would count it most important if I could make you proud of me! I would feel that my life on earth will have had some meaning if what I do from now on would make you "*quell*" or feel the pleasure in my actions.

From time to time, I seem to feel your smile when you regarded me. If I had done something unique and satisfying and I pleased you. I want to please you to this day and as you said, "Actions speak louder than words," or "Know them by their deeds."

I would hope and I will try to act intelligently, compassionately and with good humor! I will make you proud of me or I will die trying!

WHAT TIME IS IT?

July 17, 1993

Sometimes I think I'm losing it. Then I pull back from the brink. Perhaps I've had these moments and days all my life, but was immersed in daily life and had no time or need to identify the *lost child* syndrome. The *lost child*. I do not know if this is an original term or not, but no matter; it fits.

I have no direction. I have no one to turn to for direction or even discussion. I thought I was a big girl now. Of course I am, but my mind wavers at times and I forget to look at the clock and see what time it is. When am I expected to arrive?

To date, I've kept all appointments and have seemed to be totally together. I know it is a facade. I have steeled myself to pursue each day's activities and to do what must be done, but there are moments of anxiety and restlessness and impatience. What do you do with time spent so carelessly, frivolously and seemingly mindlessly?

I know it is my mind that would like to shut out and run away from the truth; the truth that I have been abandoned, not deliberately, but abandoned nevertheless. I've been left on the doorstep of life. The *lost child*, the *motherless child*, the *orphan in the storm*. All analogies, but never really reaching the core of my aloneness.

The pain within my chest is real. I've had this pain before. I remember years of this pain. I was losing my mother. For three years, I had the pain which was only alleviated when I was with her and could be close. Each time I left her, the pain returned to disappear entirely soon after she died.

Now the pain returned. The death of my husband has reinstated the pain. It began slowly and not too intense at first, but it seems to be building to a crescendo. He's been gone, dead, nine months and I cannot accept his dying. I know intellectually he is dead. Emotionally, it is another story.

I have kept busy, fortunately I have kept busy, but in the quiet times, my mind is in total chaos. I look and act normal. I know that when I am no longer "*on*," there seems to be a displacement of my persona which I have tried to accommodate.

All of this writing seems like so much gibberish and perhaps it is. I will soon be leaving to go out among my fellow inmates. This asylum, called the world, we all live in is inhabited by the keepers, the alienated, the sick and the dying. I would like to be a keeper of the flame for a little longer. I would like to burn brightly a little longer. I would like to light my way and any who join me a little longer.

I think I can, I think I must! I will have to help the lost child find herself! Easy does it, just don't push through the barrage of overwhelming thoughts! Kick back and let time perform its healing. Quit fighting the inevitable! In the end we are all losers, but let the end come as a natural, even flow. It will be okay, it will be fine. We will have lived and we will have died. It should be interesting to see the rest of our life unfold. It should be interesting!

SLEEPLESS IN SAN FRANCISCO

July 18, 1993

Up the down staircase. Down the up staircase, and so it goes up and down. I spent a day yesterday with a diverse group of people. We exchanged words, facts, reminiscences and I came away with a head full of disconnected thoughts. I can't be uninvolved and since it was impossible to become involved with so many people in so short a time, each conversation was to me, intense, but unsatisfying. I don't like tasting. I like eating, but it takes time to eat, time to savor the flavor, time to leisurely enjoy the meal and then time to digest it. Brief interchanges leave me hungry.

I wonder if other people need to be involved in the same way I do. I have been thought flighty in my time. I've danced from one conversation to another. I've juggled different topics with different people at different times.

I am still left wanting. I think my destiny is to be ever-searching and never reaching whatever it is I need. Is it love? Is it friendship? Is it recognition? I think it is all of the above, but there is a certain evanescent quality to my wandering soul. I've found a measure of contentment, but now I feel I will spend the rest of my life searching for the answer and realistically, I know there is no answer.

I am sure there are others like me on the planet. Do they find a way to subsist without having this gnawing inside? I think most people find substitutes—hobbies, religion, work and I need something else. I've always had a restless heart and I guess as long as it keeps beating, I'll just have to live with it!

DON'T LOOK!

July 19, 1993

"Mirror, mirror on the wall, who's the fairest of them all?"

I no longer have a mirror. We all live with mirrors, husbands, parents or siblings. When there is no longer a mirror in your life, you seem to disappear. I know I do.

I can see light and dark. I can feel hot and cold. But there is no one to see me. I am walking about in the world of the sightless. For the most part, people are turned inward and only have a view of themselves. We do talk to one and another, but our listening is perfunctory.

I don't want to turn inward! I want to turn inside out! I want to let the past rest in the past. I want to shed my old skin and start living my own life. I still need desperately to have a mirror to gauge my progression or dissension into the new pathways I am maneuvering. I can't see what I'm doing and there's no one to tell me how badly or how well I look or act. I'll just have to move out by the *seat of my pants* by instinct, feel or impulse.

I have been doing all of the above, but in an desultory kind of way. I will have to be more trustful of my instincts. After all, I have made it from there to here so far!

FINAL ARRANGEMENTS

July 21, 1993

I always seem to be running ahead of the pack. My mind is speeding beyond the safe limits and it is going so fast I think I will surely win the race! What race? Assorted bits of knowledge adhere to my thoughts, like flies caught on fly paper or wind-swept leaves against a fence.

When I look down I am slogging along through the muddy roads of life and I am going no faster than anyone else. Oh, to be cursed with a quick mind and slow feet! Mentally, I'm on a rampage and I haven't moved more than a few miles from my home base in months! Sometimes not even a few feet!

I must become a collector. I must arrange my thoughts and file them in order so that I can think in an orderly way. I have accomplished some positive acts, but not too much and I will continue to give myself time to assess my life and utilize my abilities in damage control.

I have taken step one. Get up! Step two! Do what I have to do! Step three, try to figure out how to get to step four. If I had an Indian name now, it would be Going Nowhere Fast!

LET'S PRETEND

July 22, 1993

There are times when I wish I had died first. I was driving home from an errand and marveled that I was still buying the odds and ends we use. I was wishing that I didn't have to pretend I was still living.

A little over nine months has passed since my husband died and I am still living. I sleep, I eat, I talk to people and move about in the world doing all the things the others do. I really wish much of the time that I didn't have to play this game of "Let's Pretend"! I'm alive and viable and smiling and seemingly happy and operational! I guess when the most important person in your life dies, it's like a car that is no longer in gear, but coasting up and down hill. It's a remembered map that you've followed so many years of your life that you just keep moving by rote.

I don't know when I will die. I don't care much, but maybe in time I will feel the joy that was once part of my persona and I can put away my mask. I won't discard the mask, but will use it on occasions when my own face grows tired of smiling. I've grown tired, very tired. I've put on the good front. I've actually found a small amount of pleasure at times.

Whenever my guard is down, I truly wish I had died first. The only sadness then would have been to leave you alone to go through what I am going through. Maybe you would have survived, but I know you seemed to be awaiting death. You were awaiting life when you went into the hospital. You were happy! You were looking forward to being able to walk better and have less pain! You were actually jolly and kidding with the nurses before the surgery. What happened? The surgery was a success and you died from the blood transfusions, the contaminated blood of someone who probably sold their blood for drugs or liquor.

We are all connected. Our lives hinge on so many small happenings. Naturally, a blood transfusion, a car out of control, a match that starts a fire and all the small and big accidents that happen. And of course, the natural disasters—earthquakes, hurricanes, floods and tornadoes. Why is my husband dead and why am I alive? Good question!

Oh, for that terrible sadness to take a back seat in my life! It does have a back seat, but it's a very intrusive back seat driver. I see you living, I see you dying. You're always with me or just over the horizon. It was a good life we had together! I just have to keep reminding myself that I was luckier than a lot of people and still am. My memories and everything surrounding me belongs to both of us. They say time heals. It does of course, but the healing is slow and I'll always have the scar.

SILENCE

July 24, 1993

It is so quiet. It is so very quiet. I open the door so I can hear the sounds of traffic and a gentle murmuring of distant noises. Within my house, everything has stopped. There are no minor creaks or groans. There is utter silence. The silence becomes a large, white noise in my ears. I've spoken aloud to myself, but the silence is pervasive and stubborn. The silence has a presence.

I look around and wonder if I'm doomed to never hear a human voice within my home. Not a temporary voice, a visiting voice, but a voice that lives here. To some who live in constant noise, the silence maybe good, but to me it is neither good nor bad. It is just silence and I live with it and maybe in time we will become friends and I will give silence a name. It is a new presence in my life and needs to be defined.

HIMSELF

July 25, 1993

I went out. I went shopping. I passed by the national cemetery where Himself is buried. I thought on my way back I will stop to go in and say hello. Attention must be paid. I cannot be this close where Himself lies buried and ignore him. I know all there is a marble slab on the ground with the wonderful name of Himself, date of birth, date of death, Star of David and military rank.

I did go in and I did say hello and I said I don't know where you are, but I know you are with me from morning to night and into my dreams. Is this what death is all about? Eternal longing for the sight, sound, touch of one you loved? At least, when I dream you touch me and I am once again the Myself I was, but the morning comes too soon!

The bleak routine of life again resumes. The day is lovely, the sun is shining. I am surrounded by all the material goods we acquired after careful searching. I still enjoy my surroundings, but the tempo has changed. It is much slower. It is harder to hear, and harder to see. Every now and then, I wonder what Himself would say to me. Maybe, "Get on with it, girl!"

I know your responses when someone would try to hurt me physically or emotionally. You would have stood up to the devil himself to protect those you loved. You were wise, compassionate and had such a fiery temper when provoked. I do miss all of the above, but mostly I miss the most wonderful presence of Himself moving around the house, sitting near me, sleeping with me, talking to me and even arguing a bit.

I will *get on* with it! How well or how long I will *get on* remains so be seen. I'll have to think on that a bit and do some more living. Out there among the gentle valley of stones, lies Himself, my beloved, surrounded by the thousands of others who have left thousands of others to mourn their passing. I am confused. I do want to know the meaning of life! Death has no meaning, absolutely none!

ANOTHER STATISTIC (IF AGE COULD TEACH, IF YOUTH COULD LEARN)

July 26, 1993

Statistically, people are living longer now. Statistically, I will be one of them. Whether this is a positive observation, probably not. Statistics are cold, lifeless facts. Our lives are filled with facts and figures having no bearing at all on the quality of life.

We're submerged and drowning in statistics, but how many of us can swim? I, myself can only float; not well, and when an unknown sound invades my ears, I go under, I am not even able to float, and have to scramble madly to something on which to cling. I've been drowning many times.

Now we get to drowning: drowning in drink, drowning in sorrow, drowning in self pity, and on it goes, the drowning! Statistically, I have a few more years, but be damned to statistics! How about the longer life that is supposedly coming my way? How do I make the most of this longer life?

You don't get medals for living longer. The papers are filled with the additional cost to the younger crowd that we old codgers will be. We don't really seem to have much merit, except we're alive.

How do you take a statistic and turn it around so that it has human value? I personally think that we should somehow use our mellowed wisdom to retrieve our self-worth and become productive in depth. I haven't thought it through yet, but it seems that we, the aged ones, have such inner strength and such broad knowledge of life, it should be bottled in some form and labeled "Life's Spirit," or packaged as "Home Girl's Kit," a how-to product to enable those who come after us to be provided with instructions of how to do the best with what you have.

It would be valuable to instill this brand of optimism and realism into the fabric of life, no matter how long you live. Statistically, this will not make much of a change in longevity, but philosophically we could go down as the Women of Reason.

KEEP ON GOING

July 27, 1993

The longer I live, I realize the longer I've lived. It seems that my life has been one long, mellow walk in the sun, through the shade, down the hills and up again. It has been so mellow!

I don't know how to really describe a long life. It was full, not full enough and yet it seemed to have suited me. My clothes are a bit tight like my life, but I still feel quite content in my skin. I see around me so many unhappy, discombobulated folk, so many searching and not finding; never being in tune with the music of life. I, myself, probably didn't hear the music when I was busy turning the pages of days, but now that I can savor the time more quietly, I realize that I've had a *good,* long walk.

I have to emphasize "good." If it all ends tomorrow, I will have no regrets, I did all I could and loved all I could and the good in my life is the loving and the doing.

To be aware is truly a wonderful feeling and I am aware. There might have been times that my vision was limited to the moment, but it always returned. Even in retrospect I saw what had happened and the whys and the wherefore of life.

Maybe I'm too accepting, but that is not really true. I've fought for what I believed and turned my back on confrontation, not wanting to insult or be insulted. I've come a long way and I am learning something new every day. I'm learning not to do anything that displeases me. I've learned to start living alone with a user-friendly me. I'm learning to keep learning. My epitaph as of today should read, "You've finally stopped me!"

WET PAINT

July 29, 1993

I've just had my house painted and it looks grand! As I've said, "Now it looks too good for the neighborhood!" All the other houses have a dull and somewhat faded look, quite decent, but not really ready for a party. My house, on the other hand, looks dressed up and ready to go!

I would love to feel like my house looks. The only thing I can relate to is the strip of paper blocking the entrance with the words "Wet Paint" printed across it. When I picked up the morning paper carefully laid on the low brick wall, I felt quite secure looking at the "Wet Paint" tape blocking the entrance to my house.

I like the feeling that no one can come in unless I give permission and then the person would have to tread carefully. I think I've left my front door unguarded these many months since I've been alone and have been too imprudent in allowing almost anyone or everyone into my house and my life. Even after the "Wet Paint" tape is removed, I think I will leave it in place in my mind.

Too many diverse lives, words and actions are clouding my vision. I find myself listening, responding and listening and none of the words I'm hearing relate to me, what I'm feeling or what I want to know. There is just a pouring out of words. I could be one of those plastic fortune tellers in a glass box at a county fair. She has a benevolent smile and when you put money in a slot, a card emerges with your fortune.

I'm in a box with a benevolent smile and I utter a few platitudes in response to other people's queries. Simplistic platitudes; I have no answers. I really have no questions. I'm just trying to get on with my life and find enjoyment whereever I can and peace of mind is an uppermost welcome visitor. The tape stays! "Wet Paint"—Don't cross and enter my life until the paint is dry!

ON THE ROAD AGAIN

July 30, 1993

Finian came in this morning. He ate. He went out on the deck and rolled in the sun. He's been meowing in his tenor voice all morning. I think he wants to know where the master has gone. I have talked to him reassuredly and told him the "main man" in our life is gone. We are still together, but I don't seem to offer him solace. He's lying on the floor behind me and I know he's still puzzled by the disappearance of the big guy in his life.

I'm not puzzled. I feel like wailing like a banshee, myself many times! All I can do is try to keep the "proverbial" busy and not think too much or too long about the future. When your mate dies, you become an amputee. Nothing visible has been eliminated, but you are aware of inner damage to the structure that is you. There is a restlessness of trying to put the pieces together and reconstruct some viable and usable fixture that continues to look like yourself, one that acts like yourself, but you feel like an empty shell surrounded by skin and bones. Finian continues his wailing. I guess since we're in this together, he is crying for the both of us. I would wail and cry like a howling wolf if it would make me feel better, but the sounds of silence are more comforting. Soon I will be up and about my business of the day.

Again, Finian questions me. Again, I talk to him and offer words of praise and comfort. We, "thinking" animals, have no real knowledge. We only think, we think. Our creatures, our cats, our dogs—they think. They have no extraneous chores or useless ramblings to cloud their pure instinctive emotions. All their thoughts and actions are motivated by their own nature. Their desires are without guile, their actions are without premeditated planning and their love is given freely without expectations. Their sadness and mourning consume them inasmuch as death is an unknown quantity and it is impossible for them to rationalize the finality of life.

Oh Finian, my Finian, try to come to terms with what has happened to us! We have lost the most precious, the dearest being in our life. Let us both try to live with today and get on with it! I'm probably reading more into Finian's actions, but even so, he is defining how I feel and it is good to know I'm not alone

I gave him a bit more food and that seemed to do the trick. He marched away and down the stairs and through the room, through the garage and down the stairs, out into the yard to go about doing what cats do. And me, oh me, very soon "I'll be on the road again."

ANXIOUS AUGUST

August 4, 1993

August. The papers are filled with several columnists talking about August. One said that August is supposedly the dullest month of the year. People are away on their vacations and nothing happens, but _____. Another says August seems to be the month of unusual happenings. It seems to include major world crises, celebrity deaths and lots of conventions.

I will get back to my August. I've just finished having my house painted. I called it the Coral Reef, mostly reef—sand and a touch of coral, and of course a large helping of the white froth that tops the waves as it comes crashing onto the sandy beach. My August!

Well, it seems the plumbing in my kitchen, the pipes attached to the dishwasher decided this was the month to take off. Vacation time you see. So they parted and now my kitchen floor is a beach front. Wavy wood, damp rugs and it is time I took a vacation from the kitchen. It has become totally user-unfriendly!

The insurance adjuster will be here tomorrow and has assured me the policy will take care of the floor. All will be taken care of. It will be replaced and the rugs will be cleaned and the pipes will be installed correctly, together with a new dishwasher. I will be afforded the pleasure of staying out of the kitchen until the deed is done, until everything is back ship-shape.

I will be on vacation, but will only have to leave home for meals and whatever pleasure awaits me. I was not looking forward to August, but since August has become my month to make my kitchen livable again, I'll try to enjoy my time away.

It seems I should have something more valuable to contribute to August than a water-sogged kitchen and a disrupted house. Actually, I'm a bit sogged and disrupted myself, so perhaps if I try to, I will find a kinship in this accidental chaotic situation!

There will be a new batch of strangers in my home putting it back in order. I would personally have settled for a good hamburger in August, but that's how this month has turned out. On with the show!

OUT OF ORDER

August 5, 1993

Everything around me is breaking down. No, not everything. But things, inanimate objects in my home; a dishwasher whose connector pipes have blown apart flooding my kitchen, therefore enabling me to put aside all my cares and woes and recreate the kitchen, the new floors and so on. It is all so frustrating, time-consuming and enervating.

I think that I, too, am out of order. I keep doing and going and I don't want to blow my connecting pipes to life because if I'm "out of order," it will take more than a new floor and a new dishwasher to assemble the pieces.

It's truly amazing how one can keep living on a damaged internal engine. I've met many damaged people. They are all moving around with invisible scars and bandages. So many of us are "out of order," but still functioning in whatever capacity is left. I would like to get back to full power or wherever I was before I began operating at a reduced rate.

I've maintained myself and not become unbalanced by perpetual motion. I remember when I tried to ice skate in my late teens at a skating rink. Having grown up in warm climate, no ice was available. I had a very difficult time on the ice because I couldn't maintain an upright position. I never really conquered the sport.

The ice rink closed, but I did skate for a while. The trick for me was to move at a very rapid rate. The speed kept me elevated and exhilarated and I could always come to a stop by holding on to the rail. Now I, too, am keeping on the move. Maybe I can put all this right someday. "Out of order" will just apply to things and I can give myself a "In Good Working Condition, Slightly Used."

HALF A LOAF

August 6, 1993

Half a loaf is better than none. That's the old saying. I think some of the time a half loaf is not necessarily less than a whole loaf. Think upon it. A whole loaf of bread often goes uneaten and is thrown away. A whole meal is more than you want to eat, depending on the size. A whole amount of money, of course, depending on the amount, is more than you need or require for the good life.

I realized last night that the secret to my contentment has been my ability to settle for half a loaf. Enough is enough. Too much of everything and anything satiates your appetite for life.

AT THE SOUND OF THE TONE

August 7, 1993

I've been out about and back to square one. I've called this one and that one and there is no one to talk to except a machine. I have a machine, too, and at times I let my machine do the talking. What an impersonal world we've evolved to in this day and age. We have so much sophisticated technology, way beyond a telephone answering machine. I feel at times that we are all extensions of some kind of machine, which is true.

My kitchen is filled with machines; to chop, slice, grate, toast, broil, simmer, bake. And my closets are filled with tools to clean large areas, corners, steps, walls, ceilings, blinds, and tight spots, where no human hand can reach. I have machines to watch entertainment, to record entertainment. Machines to play music, to record music. Machines to tape voices.

With all this sophisticated equipment, there is still nothing that can take the place of a human hand touching my shoulder. Nothing like a real, live person's smile looking at me across the room, nothing like someone to offer me a cup of coffee or a glass of water. All in all, there is nothing like the real thing.

Loneliness is the human condition. We are all destined for loneliness, sometimes for hours, weeks, days, or even years. How do we fill our lonely times? Each in his or her own way and no matter how busy we keep, loneliness is there, always very much a part of our lives. I would hope that it doesn't defeat me! I would hope I would accept it and give it credence and give it another name.

For instance, quiet leisure time or periods of reminiscences or space to do nothing, say nothing and then digest what has gone before and plan what is to come. Loneliness! It is so tragic! Change one letter and it becomes "loveliness." I know that is stretching the definition, but now and then silence can be lovely.

Don't fight it, let it sit quietly beside you and remember how the chaotic sounds of traffic or other disruptive ear aching noise has irritated you! Then the loneliness changes its character and becomes solitude, lovely solitude.

WORDS RUN THROUGH IT

August 9, 1993

At the end of my phone conversations, I find myself reading something pithy I've written. I sometimes ask the person on the other side of the line if they would like to hear my shortened version of thoughts for the day. They are polite and say yes and I proceed to read a good-bye message about life, death or the ambiguity of life. I guess I want to share my thoughts with the world at large.

I am no Charles Kuralt or no Andy Rooney. At the end of my conversation, why do I need a wrap-up in the form of some unrealized though probably underlying philosophy of life as I see it. As an amateur armchair, pen-toting philosopher, what I have to say might be relevant to some, amusing to others, but all in all, might just be a muddle of thoughts I've strung together. Not pearls of wisdom, but a random collection of bits and pieces which when taken as a whole might be seen as something worth a few minutes of someone's time.

I must be working toward a career as a two-page journalist for people who are too impatient to think too much or too long. I, myself, am impatient. I want everything to be finished yesterday. I want to not spend too much time on details. I just want to get on with it! It, being whatever it is at the moment.

Much of the time "it" is absolutely nothing. So I write, short, brief, sometimes sensitive, sometimes intelligent, sometimes senseless, sometimes humorous, and sometimes just a jumble of words.

If I ever had a by-line, I guess I would title it "Stream of Unconsciousness" or maybe "Words Run Through It," or "Woman Walks in Her Mind," or "Waco Rambler," or "Who Am I?." What a preposterous notion that I have something to give to the world!

Great minds for centuries have given great insights into the human condition. I am just an ordinary garden variety person bumbling my way down my garden path, stopping now and then to think about the now and then.

ANOTHER BATTLE

August 10, 1993

"Oh, how I hate to get up in the morning! Oh, how I hate to get out of bed!" is from a World War I song, but it applies to me today past World War I, World War II, Korea, Vietnam, and all the assorted wars since then.

I hate to get up in the morning because it's another endless day, a busy day for the most part, even a pleasant day with nice people. I don't want to spend the rest of my life in bed, but I grit my teeth, my jaw tightens and I resume my life.

Sometimes I feel like my VCR controls. I can play, stop, fast forward, record and at the end of the day, rewind. All my buttons have been pushed each day and there is nothing that I've recorded worth reviewing or putting away to be perhaps played at a later date.

I do feel mechanical. I seem to say the right words, perform and complete whatever is necessary to function efficiently. I sit and write these words down and wonder, am I making sense that is sense of my life? It mostly seems senseless, but in an indefinable way. I find I am doing the right thing or things. Taking charge of my life, moving forward at a measured pace, but it all comes down to a long tape of figures and the summation of each day has no total amount.

Oh, how I hate to get up in the morning! I keep hoping I've been having a bad dream. I am not fooling anyone, especially myself. I still feel a deep pain in my chest which comes and goes. I know the night will come again and the morning. I know I should accept the facts of life. It's the facts of death that is such a bitch and I feel anger revisiting me.

At least anger is an emotion that can fight my inner battles, the battles of my soul. If I am this so-called strong woman, the strong me should eventually conquer anger, since anger by its very nature, self-destructs.

OF CABBAGES AND KINGS

August 11, 1993

As I was showering, the phrase "Cabbages and Kings" kept running through my mind. Lewis Carroll, a genius, who wrote "Through the Looking Glass," a very clever political satire was the author who wrote "The time has come," the Walrus said, "To talk of many things; of shoes and ships and sealing wax, of cabbages and kings, and why the sea is boiling hot, and whether pigs have wings."

I have been writing more or less of Cabbages and Kings. Random thoughts, unrelated emotions and questions which have no answers, I talk of many things. "The night is fine," the Walrus said, "Do you admire the view?"

Lewis Carroll knew exactly what he was writing. I, on the other hand, am just writing. From my vantage point, I do admire the view.

DOUBLE, DOUBLE, TOIL AND TROUBLE

August 12, 1993

"Double, double, toil and trouble." A passage from Macbeth. I don't remember the rest, but I think it was a witch's brew. I myself seem to be coming to a slow boil and then a simmer.

I feel so weary, so tired of doing all the things I've been doing. I feel as if I am behind a glass wall and that no one really hears me if I talk, and that my ears are really not registering what others are saying. I feel safe behind the glass wall. After all, I can still see, but I am so apart, so divorced, so unconnected to anyone and I wonder if others feel as I do. Probably, most probably.

I wonder why I have to write my thoughts down. I wonder why I am compelled to put this on paper. If I was still sharing my life, I could talk, but I would not be saying these words. I would be talking about daily problems and also about the past, good and bad, that we shared. So much is in the past and now I'm left alone to remember. I want to remember!

There was a lot happening back then. Many volumes of days, weeks and years and special moments. I want to remember! My husband often said, "After me, the deluge" taken from a quote from Madam de Hausset in French (during the French Revolution). "Apres nous le de'luge," "After us the deluge."

We all think, after us what is left? Could the world become inundated and washed away by time? I don't know if I agree with this, but I am overwhelmed. I am in the middle of the deluge, the flood. I am on a life raft just drifting, not really caring where the waters take me!

I am beyond sadness, just lackadaisical floating through the days. I wonder if I will ever reach land. At the moment, it is enough just to stay above the flood stage.

KALEIDOSCOPE

August 14, 1993

"Loose bits of colored glass between two, flat plates and two plane mirrors so placed that changes of position of the bits of glass are reflected in an endless variety of patterns; a variegated changing pattern or scene."

That is the definition of a kaleidoscope. I am now living this life. I've wondered why I am always so tired. I wake up tired. I go through the day tired and I retire tired. For whatever reason, I was compelled to move out through a colorful maze. Different places, different people and I am filled with the variety of colors in the spectrum of the human condition.

I am processing all the words, all the outer and interior surfaces that I see about me. When I have the opportunity for closer inspection I am amazed at the beauty among the sadness which is all about me.

We are always changing, not always perceptibly to the human eye, but we are always changing. Yesterday is gone forever and so are the yesterday people. I am a survivor of many yesterdays, but my coming out party, being entirely on my own, has brought a whole myriad of changes in my life. I have written bits and pieces of colored words on paper that are reflected in an endless variety of emotions.

I am full of many scenes and many lives. I have pushed my own life aside, except for the necessaries involved. I would suppose this extreme weariness will pass when I let my own life catch up with me. I want friendship and companionship and when I am with others, I forget what it was I left behind.

Do I have to live with myself? Of course I do, but I do not seem to have a concrete purpose anymore. I have allowed myself this kaleidoscope and all the changes it entails. I would wish I wouldn't think too much. It would be nice to skate on the surface of life. I cannot get a divorce from my yesterday, but some sort of accommodation is in order.

CONDITIONED TO WANT

August 15, 1993

I opened the paper this morning and saw an ad for a remodeled kitchen, all glistening, neat, appealing and I had that urge to have it! Another page—clothing. Another urge and so it went. I realized I've been conditioned to want.

Over the years, my mind and eyes have been dazzled and bedeviled by new, shining, colorful things. Big and little. All the way from ships to slips. The ad agencies have done a number on me and I'll admit I have been a willing victim. Fortunately, I have not gone totally overboard, but my house and closets and drawers are filled with fulfilled wants, some never used.

If the medium is the message, the purchase is the purchaser. I think most of us fall happily into the world of wants. It keeps us occupied by the sound and light show of material things and blocks out our view of our destiny.

As I near the last years of my life, I know more clearly what I want and have only wanted and will always want. I want the closeness of someone to love and be loved in return. I want to see the face I love, the smile I love and even argue, disagree with who I love.

We are conditioned to want things, but I don't recollect ever being conditioned to want people; how very odd that we've not been reminded, even coerced if necessary, to learn the lesson of caring for another human being, singular and plural. I, myself, am entranced by people. They are the most desirable objects on the shelves of life. They are each in their own way glistening, appealing and colorful.

I cannot put them all in my house, closets or drawers which makes them all the more valuable. We can own things, but not people. They come and go through our lives and I enjoy each moment spent with most and will put away memories in the closet of my mind.

Now and then I find myself smiling at something said long ago or felt sad and nostalgic at an incident shared in years passed. Time is running out and I want to hold tight as long as possible to each and every person before they all slip away.

HAPPY BIRTHDAY!

August 16, 1993

Today is a birthday. My grief is ten months old. It is a very young grief. It hasn't even learned to walk yet. It still stays very close to me and needs much attention and care. Sometimes I wish it would get older and move out of the house and be on its own, but realistically I know there will be long periods of being frustrated, restricted and totally consumed by its needs.

Grief is a very demanding child. I can't remember how I felt before grief was born. I'm sure I had many moments and days of uneasy feelings, but all in all, one day passed pleasantly into another. Now each day is a challenge, a huge obstacle to squeeze past in order to move into the next day and the next. This young grief is ever present, always needy and I must be on duty ever vigilant to guard its presence.

In two months, I will light a candle for its first year and each year afterward for as long as I can. How can an emotion have such a strong life-like presence? Of course, it represents life, ergo, grief and life are one.

ARTS AND FLOWERS

August 17, 1993

Oh, what a beautiful morning! Oh, what a beautiful day! There are many beautiful flowers and much is blooming. I am, too!

I feel a glow in my face. Despite the deep loss in my life, I feel the surge of a blossoming inside. Possibly only a small bud which when the petals open will only be a small insignificant flower, but it will be a flower.

I'm going to a lecture on art later today. Art is such an all encompassing word. There are so many forms of art. I like the impressionist. I admire the old masters. I like some of the abstract, sometimes senseless array of colors. We are surrounded by art. I look out my window and see art, the sky, the hills, the clouds, the fogs, the skyscrapers, the streets and I see art.

I see folk art each day; faces of people, movements and still life. We are surrounded by art and by flowers. What a shame it will be when we leave this world! But how lucky we have all been to have spent our life in this enormous gallery!

TOWER OF BABBLE

August 22, 1993

I am surrounded, surrounded by voices from many countries, many stories, many characters. All of them interesting, intriguing and each in their own way deserves at least space in the bookcase of my mind.

I am filled with the retelling of years spent in so many corners of the world, passages through time and a finality that time is running out. I run internally, trying to bring the words and emotions together in some semblance of order. I am, I think, totally disorganized, but how can one person understand or relate to other voices in other rooms of life?

I am flattered that so many share so much with me, but sometimes the sounds are overwhelming. I feel I must retreat and slowly, methodically file and arrange my thoughts and my perceptions. The silence around me has the loudest voice of all because it speaks only to me and about me and I don't want to listen. I have nothing to say to myself, but the mundane.

Daily movements that take no mental energy are my companions, my silent friends. At the end of each day, I am left alone, tired enough to sleep is welcome. Scurrying mouse-like thoughts, I push back in their holes. I doubt if I will ever be who I thought I was, but the "tower of babble" has given me a new identity and a new wardrobe.

I am wearing words of many colors and there is a free flow of thoughts and memories between each of us. I weary more easily now. I am older, but I am constantly being revitalized by those around me. Life is such a wonderment! How I will miss it!

DARK THOUGHTS

August 22, 1993

I have a very strong feeling that I'm going to die; not today, not tomorrow, but soon. It sounds like some of the lines from the movie Casablanca "..not today, not tomorrow, etc." Why this internal melodrama today on a beautiful, sunny, warm day is beyond me? I'm healthy. Why do I think my number is coming up? Why do I think of "nada"? Why is the grim reaper following me around today? Who asked for him?

I'm not ready yet. Maybe someday, maybe in a tomorrow years away. What is it doing around me today? If Mel was here, he would say "what's the big deal? When you die, you die." Okay Mel, I'm going out. I'm visiting and having dinner out. Mel would say "..that's right up your alley, you love to go out, gai gezunterhait."

Okay, I'm going and when I come home I want this dark cloud to be gone. Away—away—away down south in Dixie. Now I'm singing songs. I will wave my witch's wand. Go—go, dark spirit of death. I'll let you know when I'm ready, maybe!

NO LONGER PLURAL

August 23, 1993

When *we* became *I*, the whole universe changed. Everything is the same and nothing is the same. I still start out each day with "we." From what shall we have for breakfast and now by the end of the day the "I" has become almost non-existent. I don't care much about "I."

I do my best with the singular, but we were the viable, intelligent, sensitive couple. We planned, we talked, we looked and we listened to each other. No matter how kind and gracious the outside world tries to be or seems to be, there is simply no "we." I can't do anything or plan anything without considering and needing the "we" viewpoint.

Will I ever get somewhere in my thinking and realize that "I" am the only one alive now in my life? The "we" will always be a part of me, but it is so very difficult to be cut off from the nurturing "we." If a branch can be grafted onto another tree or plant, possibly my solution as uncomfortable as it seems to me, now will in the future be grafted onto another strong and healthy growth, and my need for sustenance will be satisfied.

PUSHING BACK THE CLOCK

August 24, 1993

Finian, my cat and longtime companion, was taking his morning ease on the chaise outside. The deck is adjacent to the living room, dining room and kitchen. One long room, one long deck. He had finished his breakfast. I had the radio on and he heard a deep male voice. He jumped off the lounge and walked to the open door.

I knew; he thought the master's back. He keeps reminding me of how much he misses the man in his life. We often forget the creatures in our life have the same long memories as we do. He is now laying contentedly on the floor behind my chair. He does not do this often in the daytime hours. He is either hoping and waiting for the reemergence of the man who loved him so much or maybe he is trying to comfort me. Either way, the two of us are joined in common memory and uncommon love.

Finian just got up and walked toward the hall; bedroom on one side, den on the other. He stood there expectantly waiting for the man long gone these many months to reappear. After a few minutes, he settled back into a sort of sad acceptance and descended the stairs to go out and lay at the back door and take the air.

I, too, am settling back into a sort of sad acceptance. I, too, will descend the stairs and begin another day. As I told someone yesterday, my mother used the phrase "pushing back the clock." I always thought she meant the opposite since clocks don't go counter clockwise. I think I've been "pushing back the clock." I want time to go backward. I want life to be what it was before it is now. I want the past. I am sure the future, as bleak as it seems much of the time, is still out there.

STUFF AND NONSENSE

August 25, 1993

I received brochures in the mail. Catalogues all with mouthwatering pictures of clothing, furniture, linens, lamps and lovely, lovely things. I feel a bit like Pavlov's dog. I've been conditioned to want these things and go forth and buy these things. All so colorful and eye comforting.

Then I suddenly brought myself up short and questioned my programmed mind. I have a house filled with beautiful things. I have closets filled with things. What will happen to these beautiful things when I leave this beautiful world? They will probably be distributed, discarded and eventually will deteriorate into possibly a recyclable heap.

My sensible self tells me that the continual buying and storing of things is a necessary diversion. I think and I know that as long as we keep wanting, we can ignore the possibility that we are not immortal. Sure, we will live long enough to enjoy new things. Sure we know we are going to die, but that is somewhere in the distance, a long, long way on another level and maybe, just maybe, our things and ourselves will be used up at the same time. Maybe all of us will disappear in a puff of smoke and hasn't it been fun to be surrounded by all that money can buy?

I feel sad, so sad that we need to immerse ourselves in material things to survive on a daily basis without facing the inevitable end that awaits each of us. I don't want to look at any more beautiful pictures of articles calling my name and saying BUY ME, or go into stores and wander along shelves and among the racks of clothes that are luring me into their arms.

I probably will keep looking and buying. Too many years of training, but at least I realize the madness of my ways and know that my things will outlive me and that the only meaning in life are people and most particularly those I love and care about. I think if only to myself I will not say "I am born to shop." I will say, "I am born to live."

How, where and why I go about my living is now my solitary decision. I do look forward to see what I do with my life. No questions asked!

PRACTICE

August 26, 1993

Practice. We don't really think about it as we wend our way down, around and through the days. We are all practicing. The only terminology that is commonly used: to practice the piano, practice dancing, practice medicine.

I ate breakfast alone this morning and I realized I have eaten breakfast alone for about a year. I have gotten up and gone to bed alone. I have done many things alone. Actually, I'm still practicing, but I'm polishing my aloneness. I'm settling myself gently in a singular state. I will be practicing all my life, but I hope each new step I take and each new endeavor will be rewarding and that I will move on and practice and become somewhat proficient in new challenges which confront all of us.

If I had not entered this state of aloneness, I would never have realized how important practice is in living. I find myself making more and more decisions, some easily and some takes a little hand to hand combat before I come up with an answer.

I am practicing decision making. I am continually practicing. I know that I will have to practice long and hard to find a way to gracefully exit this world. Now I just want to hone the new skills that are confronting me. I actually marvel at my ability to be my own man/woman.

I've spent years practicing and I had excellent teachers. Sometimes I think, is this what it means to grow up, to be mature? I don't think so! I think we are always growing, always maturing. Our practice prohibits us from becoming stalemated.

I do find satisfaction in practicing and I am reaping the harvest of talents that were not developed until I became dependent on myself. I will be a student all my life. I will be learning all my life. As the old cliché says, "Practice makes perfect." That's not quite true, but it's about as close as we are going to get.

I'm getting my house in order, literally and figuratively. It's a tough job, but somebody has to do it!

GETTING STARTED OR LIGHT MY FIRE

August 27, 1993

I don't have much *fire in my belly.* I don't have and never did have any ambition to go out and slay the dragon. I never wanted to be rich or successful. I really don't know what I wanted to be. Existentially would be a good adverb to use about myself. I was because I was. I am because I am. Just because there was no *fire in my belly* doesn't mean that there were not glowing embers, waiting to be fanned and ignited.

I have the ability to warm chilled bodies, the ability to keep a small fire burning for myself and other sad and restless souls, and the embers that are always glowing are constantly reproducing. I've always felt this life source or energy within me. It has annoyed me at times. I've wished to be more placid and passive at times.

I am releasing this volcanic ash of my embers and now and then I see the resulting conclusions of a day spent erupting with sparks lighting here and there. Subsequently, new fires are started and small glows are seen from other sources. I am not necessarily the keeper of the flame, but I am one of the smoldering coals that is no doubt necessary for keeping alive. I will, no doubt, go out in gigantic burst of flames, which I am planning, but for the nonce I'll keep the home fires burning and anywhere else that requires my services.

FRIDAY NIGHT CAT

August 28, 1993

Finian stayed out all night. It's been very warm, actually hot and he needs to have a night out occasionally. As he gets older he doesn't need too much night life, but on an exceptionally warm night, he still enjoys the sights and sounds of the cool darkness.

I, on the other hand, have always in the past been a Saturday night girl (woman). Even if I didn't go out, I had the incessant urge to do something on a Saturday night. There are songs about Saturday night, conversations about what to do on Saturday night. It has become the night to howl, to play, to dance, to just do your own thing among other Saturday night people.

I am now staying home on Saturday night. Mostly staying home. It's still out there, full of fun and laughter, but no longer do I have the unyielding urge to partake of Saturday night festivities. I still want the fun and laughter. That hasn't changed, but I have changed in that any night for me can be Saturday night. My nights are interchangeable. Fun on Tuesday night is equivalent to any other night. I heard a line dialogue on a new sitcom last night. One woman says to another, "How can you laugh at something so serious?"

The other woman replied, "I have to laugh at sadness or problems. I'm Irish!"

I must be Irish too, not by birth, but temperament. All in all, a smile feels good and when someone returns your smile, you have a double dip of pleasure.

QUALITY OF LIFE

August 30, 1993

I just realized I have been hearing these words over the air, through the air and out of mouths of people in and out of the medical profession. What does it really mean? When a person can no longer walk, but can still think and feel, doesn't his or her life have quality? If a person is unemployed, has his or her quality of life lessened?

I hate this expression. It is a cover-up for failure, not by the person whose *quality of life* has been diminished by reduced health, income, etc. But the failure of the pundits who use it as an excuse for turning their backs on these so-called "failures." The quality of life is life. As long as we are knowing, feeling beings we have quality, unmitigated importance to ourselves and those around us.

The phrase "quality of life" has been a catch phrase for no longer paying attention to the real *quality*—life. Life, in any form, in any condition, is life and should not be filed under a catch-all turn of words. All of us who are alive have quality. I, myself, have been caught up in the words and have thought. Oh, well if his or her *quality of life* has been depleted to such a reduced stage, possibly he, she, or they should be given the opportunity to choose between life and death. No way! No way do I agree with this! Under only the most adverse circumstances do I agree. When the brain no longer functions or the body is racked with intolerable pain, then and only then is the *quality of life* without quality.

How do we get conned into all these catch-phrases thrown at us night and day? *Quality of life.* Then there's the *dysfunctional family* which would cover probably a billion people. Then "*passive aggressive*," another million. "*Self actualized.*" Ho! Ho! Ho! "*Chemically dependent*," words to live by. We are all *chemically dependent* in some form or another. I guess what I'm trying to say is—Call a spade, a spade!

CHEWING IT OVER

August 30, 1993

I have been chewing a sugarless gum for the past couple of years. I didn't always have the daily habit of chewing, but once you get your teeth into it literally, it gives your mouth a workout. So sugarless, being the lesser of two evils, gum with sugar or gum without. So I buy and chew, and chew, and chew sometimes for five minutes. Sometimes longer, but it seems on a daily basis. I couldn't find the sugarless variety that usually inhabits my mouth, so I bought another brand.

Woe is me! This gum is totally inconsistent with my personality. I chew, I think like all gum-chewers. But this new brand is trying to commit suicide in my mouth! If I don't keep up a steady pace, it begins to soften and weaken and I feel it will totally disintegrate to be absorbed by the fluids in my mouth!

It is one of the most unnerving things I've experienced in my mouth. Most foods seem to have a pleasant time being masticated. Most drink goes down easily, ice cream melts deliciously down my throat, even cough drops move about and slowly dissolve. This new sugarless gum has a mind of its own and I have to chew rapidly and steadily and then eject it from my mouth.

How frustrating to be undone by a stick of sugarless gum! It just goes to show you, it's the little things in life that are the most annoying. I can deal with most of the big things one way or another.

Pardon me for the moment, I'm getting rid of this strange substance that has taken on a life of its own and wants out or down and I'm going to give it a reprieve and myself of course, and deposit it not so gently into the garbage can.

I guess the lesson to be learned from this is don't take on anything you can't chew!

RETREADS

August 31, 1993

The last day of August! My mind keeps reeling and wheeling and the word "retread" keeps popping up in my haphazard thoughts. Retread. The word to me has been used to retread a tire. A smooth, worn tire that has become a hazard in driving. So if you can afford it, you buy a new one or if you are a little on the shorts, you buy a retread.

I don't even know if they sell tires that are retreaded anymore, but once they were available. A little more rubber was added to the worn surface and the tire was safe and usable again and you could proceed on your journey, around the block, across town or wherever your car and you have decided to go.

Retread. Not new, but additional miles added. I guess the metaphor that has been wandering in and out of my consciousness is that I have apparently been retreading myself to continue my journey like the tire that is put back in use. Neither of us will go the distance of a new, unused and fresh out of the box, but we are both good for many miles.

If we don't go over too many roads or across too treacherous terrain, we do have miles to go before we sleep. I don't particularly like to categorize myself as a worn out anything, but I have to admit, I am a bit frayed at the edges.

If antiques of any sort have value, paintings and sculptures, and aged wine, why not people who have been mellowed and polished by the years to a patina not available in anything new and untested and untried?

We, the retreads, have made many journeys and we are still running, walking, or whatever ability has remained to keep us operating at full power. Our physical power might be lessened, but our mental power has grown and improved and it is so important to go on and about and continue to leave our "footprints on the sands of time."

LIGHTS OUT

September 1, 1993

Well, you see it is this way. When God or whoever made me, He forgot to install a turn-off switch. That light that shines in all of us some of the times and in others, most of the time, shines in me twenty-four hours a day, three-hundred and sixty-five days a year.

I have the ability to dim the light, but it keeps burning, even during my sleeping hours. There are times when my inner light totally consumes me and the delight and pleasure of life is so bright, I am dazzled and then it subsides to a steady glow and I feel the warmth about me, the friendship, and of course, the sadness.

It doesn't matter even when I am alone for along periods. The inner light keeps flickering and teasing me back to turn up the switch and look around me and see what else is out there waiting to be discovered or who is out there to become acquainted with and involved with and a new adventure is waiting, always waiting for me.

My light, at times, is like a torch and other times like a candle. It keeps leading me past the shadows and around the corner of days. I am sometimes so weary, I would like to snuff out the candle, blow out the torch and turn off the light. Obviously I don't have the ability. It's been a very important ingrained part of my psyche.

I have to sum all of this up and I have no words to really clarify this internal energy that invaded me back before I could make choices. If I had a choice, I think I would have chosen to be what I am. Therefore, I am. How profound this all sounds, but it is the truth as I know it and the truth has always been my ally.

LOVE IN THE MORNING

September 3, 1993

I just picked up my cat, Finian. It's morning and I thought why are we so busy that we don't have time for love in the morning? I put him in my lap and he settled down and I thought most of us don't have time or don't make time for love in the morning. Finian never sits in my lap in the morning.

He's up, a fast breakfast and a day on the road. His day consists of going down the stairs, across the deck where he gazes out at his world or down into the yard among the weeds and bushes where he spends hours exploring or possibly ruminating about the events in his life. He surveys his kingdom and then no doubt settles down for one of his interminable naps.

This morning, I hauled him upstairs and plopped him on my lap and said, "How about a little love in the morning?" He reluctantly agreed and he's still laying passively and waving his plumelike tail gently. This won't last long. He is trying to accommodate my wishes, but eventually either the army of fleas will attack him and he will need to give them what for (in his case a good scratch and a kick) or I will move more than he feels necessary and that will be the end of my love in the morning.

Remembering way back when we go to school, we have to get ready, no time for much else in the morning. Then on to growing up; kindergarten, elementary school, junior high school, high school, college and then the JOB. Getting a job, working on a job and there is no time in the morning to quietly contemplate love.

Then for some, marriage and children. Mornings are filled with everything but love. Sure, the activities of daily life require care and effort, but I am talking about love, warm, silent love. Just a touch, a caress. Something so small in comparison to the busy, busy schedule of our lives, but so very important. As the word in use this decade, nourishing (food for the soul).

Love in the morning. It isn't until we get older and school is a distant memory and working is something we've filed away under retirement and we are left with time and many, many times, we are left alone. All those years, all those busy years, interspersed with some fun, some travel, some illness and now we have our quiet mornings. But where's the love? We've always loved, but not the quiet morning love which at this time of my life seems to be what I need to make it through the day.

What I need is a gentle pat on the back to start another day of being. I'll just have to try to seduce my cat, Finian, to give me a little love in the early hours. It might not be the answer to my mornings, but it is a lot better than no love at all!

DEATH AND TAXES

September 3, 1993

I wrote out checks today for taxes. Death and taxes. The only two unchanging facts of life. Taxes. Mine is fairly simple. I have no deductions, no capital gains, no business circumventions, no free lunches. Let alone a buildup of frequent flyer miles enabling me to take friends or family around the world, around the country or just a short hop to somewhere else, a somewhere else many of us travel to.

Taxes. It's just money. The most obvious way of communication. Our shopping sprees which can cost money are our way of communicating with our desire for things. Taxes is our way of communicating with our government enabling us to have the services they provide.

I really don't know why people complain so much about taxes. Okay, so some people are feeding off the public trough. So what! Greedy people always want more and often get more, but does it matter if the rest of us have enough? I am not including the impoverished as that is a totally different problem which, if they could, they wouldn't be the down and outers. I'm talking about the middle class, the upper middle class and the upper.

Deaths, on the other hand, is no communicator. Death is the great equalizer. Death is our destiny. Death can be described in many ways, i.e., the grim reaper, overseer of departed soul and on it goes. Death is just that—death; the end, nada, nobody home, finiti.

Alas, the sad fact of life is death and I suppose if we keep complaining and bitching about taxes, death is just a word that rhymes with breath and that is the irony of the whole thing. No breath equals death. On the whole, I'd rather keep paying taxes.

COMPULSION

September 4, 1993

I have done odds and ends this morning. I've done my telephone stint. I still feel there is something wrong. I've *written* checks, paid bills and I find myself wandering through the house, up and down the stairs. What am I looking for, who am I looking for? I guess I'm just looking and not finding.

I have an uneasy, queasy feeling and I thought, ***okay, write about it; if you write about it, you'll sort it out, sort of.*** I have this compulsion to put words on paper, string beads of thoughts. I'm developing into an obsessive compulsive (but only in writing) and if it works for me, fine! If not, my words of wit and wisdom are my comfort in my advancing age.

This whole thing sounds silly when I reread it, but humor has always been my best friend! So let silly be its kid sister.

Days of fog and dozes. I feel sleepy and dizzy and weepy and fizzy (semi-internal combustion). I hope by the time I've written these sentences, my sense will return and there will be no more nonsense for today.

I'm fine, I am! I just need a little guidance to get me through today. It's not easy being your own cook and bottle washer. We all need a little help. Today, I need emotional help, which I will be receiving soon. I need someone to laugh with, to eat with and if necessary, to cry with. Whoever said "no man is an island" was one smart cookie! Of course, on the other hand, if too many boats lay anchor on my island, then there is no room for me.

Boy, am I getting into deep stuff today! Actually, when push comes to shove, I'm always in deep stuff. I just don't bring it out for display often for others or even myself. "Deep within me lies" and I can't remember the rest of the song. I think it's from "Deep in the Heart of Texas." I'm really going back to my roots now, but mostly I'm a tumbling tumbleweed. Now that's the song I really like!

REDUCTIONISM (MONDRIAN)

September 4, 1993

I don't know whether I wrote about my introduction to modern art, but it doesn't matter. I listened to a well-versed woman discussing one of those so-called modern artists. She was well-informed and I enjoyed listening to her, surrounded as I was by other senior citizens, two of whom kept dozing off.

This artist had started as a landscape painter and then evolved or, dissolved, into squares and rectangles of color, eventually each square defined by bold black lines. I was bemused by all of this and mentioned that I said he was a reductionist. My opinion, which I kept to myself, was that he was reducing something real to bits of colors which have no meaning, except possibly to himself.

At the end of the lecture, our hostess read from the huge art book, which contained many of his paintings plus an overview of his art. He was called a reductable impressionist. I was right. He was a reductionist, but not the way I viewed his art. Possibly, the artist and I would agree if he was alive and we, per chance to meet and talk, both of which would have been highly unlikely.

Most of us, if we can afford it and sometimes even if we can't, are expansionists. We accumulate worldly goods all our lives. Lots and lots of stuff. Closets, drawers, rooms of stuff. We need to be surrounded by stuff to feel secure, I think. Enough food to eat, hopefully an abundant supply. Enough chairs, sofas, stools, so we can sit wherever we want, whenever we want. Clothes, clothes, over clothes and under clothes to keep warm, to cover our bodies, to please our view of ourselves. Pictures, pots, pans, and plants.

Good heavens! We are truly expansionists! I am very secure if I depend on the stuff around me, but I am not as secure as I would wish to be. It's not the stuff that gives us true security. I hate to say it out loud, but here it goes. It's love! Good old unselfish love that is given and received by two consenting adults. Maybe I am a closet reductionist and would like my life to be reduced to only one word and one person. If this can no longer be, I will reduce my expansionist self to a more moderate level.

I am sure I will keep adding to my horn of plenty, but at a reduced rate. I will be a reduced expansionist or an expanded reductionist. Either way, I have no choice, but to do the best I can, when I can, with whom I can.

FOCUS, GROUNDED, CENTERED

September 5, 1993

Focus, grounded, centered. All words used today to define our behavior. All good terms. I have been told I am focused. I can see ahead to some extent, not too far, but ahead. It seems to me the world is out of focus. Grounded, I am grounded—down to earth—have my feet on the ground (yes and no, I have my feet on the ground), but my mind is like a butterfly or some other flying insect. It flits here and there and lands, so far safely and reviews the world or ground.

My physical self moves about in a grounded fashion, my mental self is far above the earth. Centered, whatever that is supposed to mean, Narcissist, comes to mind. Self-involved, center of my own universe. I don't think that is the usage today. Centered—in control, ability to do your own thing. Isn't it ridiculous to be analyzed, described and given respect for three little words, that can mean anything and nothing depending on their usage?

All of us, one way or another, are focused (though our view of life might be blurred or askew), grounded, as long as we are alive we are above ground. Centered—ah, centered. We are in the middle, (in the center) of what; we are centered, gather the wagons around us at a time of danger or unease. Centered, self-centered.

Words, words to live by and we do have to move away from using words as symbols of life. Words are to be used for communication, for writing plays, books and poetry. Words are to be used in the language of business, but not to define the enigmatic nature of man.

We are always changing, we are growing older and may be wiser, but we are changing. No word can adequately describe what we really are because tomorrow we could be and will be another word. I guess since we live in a jumble of sounds and voices, there are those of us who strive to make identification. If I had an identification card describing my persona, it would probably be an exclamation mark, a question mark, perhaps a comma and of course, a period. But no words!

ALONENESS

September 5, 1993

I was born to be alone. There has always been aloneness in me. I lived with my parents, but I lived alone. I've lived with someone all my life, but there was only one singular me accommodating myself to others around me. It was good not living alone. If I hadn't shared myself most of my life, my aloneness might have devoured me. Since I am *now* truly alone, I can relax in my solitude.

I still need and want people around me. They are very important. Without the sound of others and the sight of others, my identity would become too solitary even for me to bear. It's just that I know now when the world is too much with me, I can go into my own world, my alone world and hold hands with myself, symbolically speaking.

I can reassure myself, I can even flatter myself and probably the most important aspect is not having to be accountable to anyone for anything. There is absolutely no one or nothing that depends on me, except perhaps my cat. Since he's a very independent creature, he only requires feeding and a lap for an hour in the evening.

Both requests I gladly bestow on this warm, furry green-eyed animal that I truly love. With my new found aloneness, I will try to finally at this late date become what I truly am and if I truly am something else, my options are always open!

ELVADA

September 7, 1993

I grew up with a girl named Elvada. She was one of a large family. She was my neighbor and friend from about age thirteen to seventeen, at which time I left the neighborhood, the city and the state.

I have not met too many Elvadas in my life, but this morning she comes to mind while reading the paper. I'm not sure what triggered the memory, but it doesn't matter. There was always an innate honesty in Elvada. She did not see the world through rose-colored glasses. She saw the world as it was. She had no pretense, no affectations and total loyalty and fairness. Here we all were in our early teens giggling, eyeing the boys, experimenting with cosmetics and depending on our personalities, falling all over ourselves with growing up.

Elvada did not have this problem. She was always the same, always in charge of herself and always allowing each of us to be silly and sometimes ridiculous in our actions. She accepted us. She accepted everybody and their differences.

I think for those years she was very effective in stabilizing my youthful exuberance and was always the stalwart friend. No "ands or buts." I've met a few Elvadas in my life, but very few. I guess she was born with an inner peace and never deviated from what she saw was right and reasonable. The last I heard she was married and had a son and lived somewhere out in the country.

I have no idea where she is now or if she is now, but I would like to take off my hat (if I wore a hat) to the Elvadas of the world. We need more old fashioned good, honest, loyal, non-judgmental people in the world. These people are not a barrel of laughs, but they are our audience and our backbone. Here to all the Elvadas, I salute you!

DANNY BOY

September 7, 1993

"The pipes, the pipes; they are a-calling,
from glen to glen and down the mountain side.
The summer's gold and all the roses dying.
'Tis you, 'tis you must go and I must cry."

I have been hearing the pipes. I never heard them before. I don't know whether there is a hereafter or reincarnation. I don't know what happens when you die. I also know if my husband could communicate with me after his death, that it would most likely be the pipes.

He had an inordinate love of the music of the bagpipes. I have been hearing the pipes for months. I've been talking to them. That is, talking to him. At times they seem loud and persistent. I want to know what he wants or does he just want me to know he is all right?

I think he is saying, "Get on with your life, watch your step, be cautious. I am not around to protect you from those who will use you. You have to step back and be more observant now. You are alone. It's not too bad, but you cannot be as open as you are. Open the door of your heart, but keep the screen door closed until you get a good look at who and what is out there."

I have thrown caution to the wind to some extent, but I am listening to the pipes. I am now listening.

I would like to title my words, my memories, the onrushing thoughts that keep tumbling from my mind "The Pipes are Calling," as I'll be here in sunshine and in shadow. Oh, "Danny Boy," oh, "Danny Boy," I loved you so!

SOMETHING NEW

September 11, 1993

I had new shades made for my living room. I have a wall of windows. I just realized my shades are like my wallpaper and my wallpaper is like my shades, ergo, I now have a wallpaper room! It's rather amusing sitting in a paper room. I've heard the term "paper moon" and of course "paper boy," but I am sure there are other people somewhere living in paper rooms and I don't mean the street people living in large cardboard boxes. When I think upon it, mull it over, we all live in fragile surroundings, be it in the woods, in the cities or on mountain tops. Something is going to get you sooner or later, be it a natural disaster or the inevitable dissolution of our physical being.

At the moment, I am living in my paper room surrounded by an assortment of colorful tables, chairs, pictures and other collectibles. My wallpaper room seems very sturdy to me. It seems to have a very balanced, stable aura. Each wall matches the other. It's a comfortable marriage of two look-alikes, appreciating the similarity.

I, on the other hand, appreciate diversity more. Different people, different viewpoints, different foods. There's more excitement and stimulation in differences, but at the moment in my paper room, I am enjoying the stability of the walls that surround me.

As the French say "Viva 'la difference." I will have to unearth some phrase or quote which says "Vive ut vivas," live so that you may (truly) live. Or from the Latin "Humani nihil alienum," nothing that relates to man is alien to me. I will now close this diatribe about my newly refurbished paper room with a Polish expression "I mucha nie bez bnzucha," even a fly has got a belly!

DOWN FOR THE COUNT

October 11, 1993

I have had a year of aloneness. A year spent in introspection, escapism and a continuous rampage of chasing shadows. I feel like a boxer who has been on the circuit too long and had too many events. I've been knocked down, got up, and knocked down again and again, and have resumed an upright posture again and again.

Today, I think I'm *down for the count.* The winner is ____! It is not me. I've been a contender and I think it's time to turn in my gloves. I am tired, so very, very tired. I have to stop fighting and go into retirement. I tried my best to stay in the ring, but it's time to move on. What lies ahead might be less exciting than the challenges I have been confronting this past year, but when the body is tired, the spirit has to stop pushing and let you rest.

I don't know what's around the corner and at the moment I don't care. A new career move is definitely in the works and if it turns out to be nothing more than looking at the clouds or watching the grass grow, I will go for it! Slow and easy does it!

If I want to go out in style, I have to revamp my act. No more ingenue parts, give me the rocking chair roles. "Old rocking chair's got me!" Maybe, I'll settle for something a little more sophisticated, like a big couch. But no matter what, I'm getting out of the ring and hanging up my gloves.

THE DYING TIME

October 12, 1993

This date last year I was in the middle of the dying time. As the old adage goes, "there is a time to live and a time to die." This was my husband's time to die. I didn't really know this. I knew he was very ill, but he had gone in for a routine operation which was successful, but he was dying and now almost a year later, I am reliving the dying.

How odd, what a strange dichotomy. I am living and he was dying. No one can face the inevitability of death. I can't, intellectually, of course. Intellectually, everything is possible. Emotionally, no. Emotionally, the possible is impossible. I will spend a few more weeks in the dying time and then my new year will start.

My new year will be the day after death. I will try to celebrate life, my life and those around me. It will never be the happy new year of the past , but it is the only new year I have now and I must try to make the most of it.

The dying time. It is the late fall. Summer is long over and in some parts of the country, the ground is covered with dead leaves. Trees have shed their greenery. Grasses are brown and cold winds begin to blow. It is proper to die in the fall, it is our alliance with nature. We live side by side and when we leave, it is fitting that the season complements our return to the soil.

Oh, how sad is the dying season! My heart is filled with dead leaves and cold winds, but I still remember your warm smile and your gentle touch. We will all join you soon. Rest in peace, my fallen warrior, the wars of life are over for you, but I have a few more battles ahead. I hope I am as adept and victorious as you were in fighting the good fight. No matter, I had a good teacher and should do well enough.

EXIT EASILY

October 13, 1993

I think I died a long time ago. I think I was seven. I didn't die, of course, but I think part of me died. I did all the things children do. I went to school, I played, I grew up or at least part of me did. I got married, I got divorced. I played the single scene. I married again and now I am waiting for the rest of me to leave. I laugh too easily. I'm too accepting. I don't worry enough. I don't think I care enough though I do like the caring at times.

All of the above are not the personalities of the living beings around me. There is a serious flaw in my make-up. I need to be continuously on. I need to have an audience. I need others around me to give me identity. I need to fly, verbally speaking. I have very little fear because when you are already dead, the problems of the world no longer matter.

Now and then, I feel my feet reach down and touch the soil of reality, but mostly when I'm not talking or doing, I'm drifting, going absolutely nowhere. I pretend I'm alive most of the time. I think most people think I'm carefree, at times scatter-brained, a funny, pleasant person.

I am to a certain extent all of these things, but mostly they are a cover for the dead me, the me that has very little value in the scheme of life. The me who doesn't care if she goes to sleep or wakes up. Since I do wake up, I continue my mad scramble through the day, finding no peace, bits of fun and the ghoulish awareness that I am not really alive.

I wonder if I am writing these morbid words out of sadness, ennui or enlightenment. No matter, I truly feel a lack of the life force. Once I am gone, it will be as if I were never here. This is not an unhappy feeling. It is just a fact. I know sooner or later everybody dies and sooner or later are forgotten, but this is different.

I am the bright flame and once I've been extinguished, the flame ceases to exist. How long I will burn brightly, I don't know, but a flame is an inanimate object and I am that object. I hope I've warmed a few that were close to me. If so, I will have served my purpose. How very strange to know you are dead and continue to live! How strange!

OFF TO SEE THE WIZARD

October 16, 1993

The earth-tone men. I am sure there are earth-tone women too, but I spent a few minutes yesterday with a man. He was dressed in blue jeans, tired green shirt, and had deep circles under his basset hound eyes. He is a professional man and goes to court for all the right things; civil rights or liberties, harassment cases, disability claims and all the underbelly cases of the legal profession. He never smiles. I know he must be a conservationist and if not belong, at least support all the "Save the ____" causes.

I was thinking about all the earth-tone people, i.e., all the well meaning, joyless _____ whose very outward dress reflects the colorless, bleakness of our lives. I respect them. I commend them, but I could never join their ranks. I, too, support all the worthy causes, but not actively. I would have to spend all the hours and days of the rest of my life to protest the inequities of our society. I need to wear bright clothing to give my body a chance to sing and say, "Look at me." I'm happy even when the happiness is only the film on the surface.

Most of all, I need to laugh and find humor in the most unhappiest of situations. I cry inwardly, but refuse to show that face because I have a mirror that would reflect the sadness back and I refuse, I simply refuse to allow myself to be immersed in the "woe is me."

I am no Pollyanna. I don't look for the good in people. I accept them as they are, expecting no more or no less than they offer. Today, is the first day of the rest of my life and I will continue to live it the only way I know how, which is as I've always said, "Follow the yellow brick road." Where the road takes me, I go, and if I don't land up in Oz and I don't see the wizard, at least I will die trying!

HERBAL TEA

October 20, 1993

I've been mulling now and then what I'm all about, that is, what annoys me, what pleasures me and what I really don't give a fiddler's damn about.

Starting with food, and I like food, I really get ticked off by people who request herbal tea, also no salt or sugar (unless they have a physical problem forcing them into this unhappy choice). The same goes for anything low fat. Life is low fat enough. After years of living between happy and trying times, I don't need food to become a hostile presence, ergo, I eat what I want, when I want and let the devil take the hindmost.

Now to our television viewing preferences. I am not a sports fan, but what the heck, those that enjoy, enjoy. I like good and some bad sitcoms. I hate "disease of the month television movies," or "crimes of the year or whatever." If I want to see suffering, I can always turn on television and watch starving people or an assortment of wars where people kill each other.

I like going out, but I like staying home. I like to travel, but the older I get, the pleasure has lessened. It isn't because I've seen it all. I think it becomes a chore to see. The packing, the planning, the plane rides, the airports, the hotels and when I finally reach my destination, I have assorted memories of getting there and a consuming annoyance of the return trip. So the in between, the place, the sights and sounds of other places is only a small portion between two huge slices of the sandwich called the "trip."

I guess what I mostly like is the quiet within my own walls and the companionship of friends and assorted acquaintances laughing and talking and indulging in small games. I enjoy sharing meals in and out of homes. I enjoy any sitcom on television that has a dog in it. I still enjoy reading, though I don't have the staying power of reading for several hours that I used to do in the good old, bad old days. I like music sometimes. I think sooner or later I will enjoy it more. Just now it keeps stirring up memories that make me feel so sad.

Of course, I like my cat. He's been my companion for over twelve years and I feel he is the only one left that I can truly love and be loved by. He's not that lovable, but I love him anyway. He gives me his fifteen minutes of love late at night when he climbs on my lap and curls into a big, furry ball. It's nice to say, "I love you" to something and really mean it.

I like knowing that I have the freedom to go anywhere I want to and do anything I please. The other side of the coin is that I don't have to do anything or go anywhere if I don't want to either. This list could probably continue for several pages and if I wait a few more minutes I could add to the list.

I suppose a summation is in order. Basically, I have no strong dislikes. I really give everybody, including myself, space to be whatever they are. I just have preferences. I suppose mostly I'm glad I was born, I'm glad I'm the me I am. I would have liked to be more, but have no idea what the more should have been or could have been. I guess you could call me a "satisfied customer."

HALLOWEEN

October 31, 1993

I've come to the *time between,* which coincidentally rhymes with Halloween. I've been out searching, reaching, touching, but the only feeling at the end of the day is weariness, numbing, mindless, senseless ennui. It is a mixture of physical and emotional, but the sum total adds up to "bone tired."

I think perhaps it is time for the "in between," a time to reflect and inspect. A time to go below the speed limit and be the observer instead of the driver. A time to muse and if lucky, bemused. When I turn the dial in my mind, I will perhaps find at least solace in being alone. I can change my inner channels, but I am not honed into anything for any longer than I choose.

Solitude is not my enemy and has never been. I find it more challenging than the running around and about, mostly like the spinning cages we used to see of guinea pigs. The ceaseless, sameness and very little satisfaction. We all live in spinning cages, but have the ability if we are aware enough to slow the pace and truly appreciate not only what we have, but the world around us.

It is a beautiful world, but you can't see very far or very much if you are speeding through life. On the other hand, one shouldn't spend their life in introspection. There is no bottom to the pit of our essence. We just have to walk lightly along the brink and not fall into self pity.

We don't even have to know ourselves to a great extent. Just give ourselves breathing room and then proceed at a moderate movement and move gently within our skin, taking "time out" not to use the old cliché "smell the roses," but perhaps "don't smell the rat" either. I truly believe, I did the best I could, but I need strength to continue the trip, so the "time between" will replenish the energy needed for my voyage.

MY DYING TIME, PART II (Continuation of October 12, 1993)

December 10, 1993

There comes a time when we stop living and start dying. I am now in the dying time. The living was filled with many things; work, problems, illness, dancing, cooking, cleaning, buying and trying to make the best of each worst.

Now in the dying time, all of the above has minimal meaning and is of minimal interest. Most of the problems that were unsolved remain unsolved. Cooking, cleaning, and even buying (though this still engenders a degree of excitement) are put aside and only the fact of illness remains to be acknowledged when and if it becomes significant.

The dying time. Time spent reminiscing, time spent savoring the accumulated material successes we have achieved, but all the while becoming aware how ephemeral are the days and trying not to get bogged down in self pity. We come face to face with the dying time when our spouse of many years dies.

We never thought we were eternal, but now we know the sad truth. I look around and truly appreciate everyone and everything I know and have, but there is a continual undercurrent of fear that time is running out. Was the past really as good or bad as I remember?

It doesn't matter, but for the fact, the past is what I am all about. The future holds some promise in small ways, but the past is what formed me, comforted me and honed me into this person who is now dying.

I guess at this point in my life I am a follower. My grandparents, my parents and my husband who went before me have paved the way into the great unknown and since all of them lived bravely and courageously. I hope I have the ability to leave with the same dignity they did.

This is not supposed to be a sad essay on dying. I am only stating the truth as I see it and if the saying "the truth shall set you free," perhaps I will feel free to spend the rest of my life without inner conflict and only inner peace.

Here's how to order additional copies of

Seduction of Silence

by Helen Lewison

Please send $14.95 per copy + $3.50 shipping for 1st copy; add $1.50 shipping for each additional copy to the same address. Books are shipped by 1st class mail. California orders: Please add $1.12 sales tax per book for all orders shipped to California addresses.

Your Name (please print) ______________________________

Address to send book(s) ______________________________

____

No. of copies ordered ______ Amount enclosed __________

Please make checks payable to Helen Lewison and mail to

Helen Lewison

Mrs. Helen J. Lewison
86 Aloha Ave.
San Francisco, CA 94122